I

Race and Racialism

Race and Racialism

edited by
SAMI ZUBAIDA

Foreword by T. B. Bottomore

TAVISTOCK PUBLICATIONS
London · New York · Sydney · Toronto · Wellington

First published in 1970
By Tavistock Publications Limited
11 New Fetter Lane, London EC4
Printed in Great Britain
In 11 pt Monotype Plantin 2 pts leaded
by Richard Clay (The Chaucer Press), Ltd.,
Bungay, Suffolk

S B N 422 73620 1 (hardback)
S B N 422 73630 9 (paperback)

© The British Sociological Association 1970

Distributed in the USA
by Barnes & Noble, Inc.

Contents

Editorial Note

The papers in this volume are a selection from contributions to the Annual Conference of the British Sociological Association held at University College London, 26–29 March 1969, on the theme of 'The Sociology of Race and Racialism'. I wish to take this opportunity to thank the contributors and discussants for a stimulating and lively conference. Contributions from the official discussants and from other participants are not included in this volume. I have tried in the Introduction to take up some of the main issues raised in the discussions.

Contributors

SHEILA ALLEN, born 1930. Studied at the London School of Economics, B.A. (Sociology) and postgraduate Anthropology. Assistant Lecturer in Sociology, University of Birmingham 1959–60; Lecturer 1960–1. Lecturer in Sociology, University of Leicester, 1961–5; Senior Lecturer in Sociology, University of Bradford, 1966.

Author of several articles and *Coloured Minorities and British Society* (forthcoming).

Currently engaged in research on the employment patterns of coloured workers.

MICHAEL BANTON, born 1926, Birmingham. Studied at London School of Economics, B.Sc.(Econ.); University of Edinburgh, Ph.D., D.Sc. Assistant in Social Anthropology, University of Edinburgh, 1953–5; Lecturer, 1955–62; Reader, 1962–5. Visiting Professor of Political Science, Massachusetts Institute of Technology, 1962–3. Professor of Sociology, University of Bristol, since 1965.

Author of *The Coloured Quarter*, 1955; *West African City*, 1957; *White and Coloured*, 1959; *The Policeman in the Community*, 1964; *Roles*, 1965; *Race Relations*, 1967.

NICHOLAS DEAKIN, born 1936, Oxford. Studied at Oxford University, B.A. (Modern History), M.A. Civil Servant (Administrative Class) Home Office, 1959–63; Assistant Director, Survey of Race Relations in Britain, 1963–8. Research Fellow, Centre for Multi-Racial Studies, University of Sussex, since 1968; Director, Joint Unit for Minority and Policy Research, 1969.

Co-author of *Colour and Citizenship*, 1969, editor *Colour and the British Electorate 1964*, 1965.

Currently engaged in planning research programme in race relations for multi-disciplinary research unit linking Institute of Race Relations with University of Sussex.

JOHN R. LAMBERT, born 1940, London. Studied at the University of Sussex, B.A.; the Institute of Criminology, Cambridge University; Research Officer, Institute of Race Relations, 1966–7; visiting exchange student Columbia University Law School, 1967–8; Senior Research Associate, Centre for Urban and Regional Studies, Birmingham University, 1968.

Author of *Crime, Police, and Race Relations* (in the press).

Currently engaged in research concerning race relations and housing policies.

DAVID LOCKWOOD, born 1929, Yorkshire. Studied at London School of Economics, B.Sc.(Econ.), Ph.D. Assistant Lecturer in Sociology, 1953–8, London School of Economics; Lecturer, 1958–60. Rockefeller Fellow, University of California, Berkeley, 1958–9. University Lecturer, Faculty of Economics, and Fellow of St John's College, Cambridge, 1960–8. Visiting Professor of Sociology, Columbia University, 1966–7. Professor, Department of Sociology, University of Essex since 1968.

Author of *The Blackcoated Worker*, 1958; co-author of *The Affluent Worker*, 1968–9.

JOHN REX, born 1925, South Africa. Studied at Rhodes University College, B.A., and University of Leeds, Ph.D. Held teaching posts at the universities of Leeds and Birmingham. Professor of Social Theory and Institutions, University of Durham, 1964–70. Recently appointed to the Chair of Sociology at the University of Warwick.

Chairman of the British Sociological Association since 1969.

Author of *Key Problems in Sociological Theory*, 1961; co-author with Robert Moore of *Race, Community and Conflict*, 1967. Forthcoming book, *Race Relations and Sociological Theory*.

HAROLD WOLPE, born 1926, South Africa. Studied at University of Witwatersrand, B.A. (Social Studies), LL.B. Lecturer in Sociology, University of Witwatersrand, 1949–50; Barrister of the Supreme Court of South Africa, 1954–9; Solicitor of the Supreme Court of South Africa, 1960–3; Staff-Tutor in Sociology, Delegacy for Extra-Mural Studies, University of Oxford, 1965–6; Lecturer in Sociology, University of Bradford, 1967–9; Principal Lecturer in Sociology, North-Western Polytechnic, London, since 1969.

Author of 'A Critical Analysis of Some Aspects of Charisma', *Sociological Review*, Vol. 16, 1968; 'Structure de Classe et Inégalité Sociale – principes théoriques de l'analyse de la stratification sociale', *L'Homme et la Société*, No. 8, 1968.

SAMI ZUBAIDA, born 1937, Baghdad. Studied at the University of Hull, B.A., and the University of Leicester, M.A. Lecturer in Sociology, University of Leicester, 1963–8. At present Lecturer in Sociology, Birkbeck College, London.

Foreword

T. B. Bottomore

This volume, the first in a series of annual conference papers to be published by Tavistock Publications for the British Sociological Association, marks fittingly the progress of a decade in British sociology. Since the early 1960s, not only has there been a remarkable expansion of sociological teaching and research, but the subject has come alive in a way that was scarcely conceivable ten or fifteen years ago. Then, sociology was a poor relation among the social sciences in British universities, contributed little to intellectual and political controversy, and aroused hardly a flicker of interest among the general public; now, it has assumed, in many respects, a central place in university teaching, while the work of sociologists figures prominently in the public discussion of social issues and enters increasingly into policy-making in many different spheres.

The rise of sociology can be seen as a response to changing social needs, and above all to the appearance of new types of social and political problem. In Britain, it is connected particularly, I think, with the strains and uncertainties resulting from the loss of empire and from the difficult process of adjustment to the conditions of the postwar world. But there have also been more general influences at work, affecting all the industrial societies. The growth of sociology has been stimulated by the new opportunities and dangers that rapid technological advance (in all its peaceful and warlike forms) and sustained economic growth have brought in their train. There is now, especially in the younger generation, a lively sense of the possibilities for fundamental social change, for the creation of new forms of society; and, at the same time, a widespread conviction that the development of each society, and of the whole world community, needs to be more deliberately guided and planned – that men have to establish, in common, a more rational control over their own social life if they are ever to realize all the benefits of their technological mastery of nature. Sociology provides, however imperfectly as yet, an essential framework of ideas and theories within which the major problems of industrial societies – and increasingly, those of the industrializing societies – can be formulated, argued about, and seen in their relation to political ideologies and social movements.

Of course sociology is not the only form of response to the contradictory experiences of hope and disillusion, promise and frustration, in the advanced industrial countries. There have been many cultural innovations, from the brief appearance of the angry young men and television satire, to the emergence of hippie communities, the cult of pop music, and the idea of a 'counter-culture'. These have tended to promote a movement towards greater 'permissiveness', especially in middle-class spheres of life, to diffuse a more critical view of established institutions, and to oppose authoritarian elements in the social structure of Western societies. New styles of political thought and political action have worked, to some extent, in the same direction. Sociology itself has been affected by these changes in the cultural environment. The expansion of the subject has been accompanied by a greater readiness to engage in social criticism, and to forsake the uncommitted attitude, the posture of 'value-free science', that characterized the preceding decade. It has become fashionable, indeed, to talk about a 'critical' or 'radical' sociology. But if the sociologist has a highly important intellectual role as a critic of society, he has too the equally important responsibility of describing and explaining the social world as it exists, while remaining aware of all the difficulties that surround the notion of the 'objectivity' of social phenomena. He is not simply a critic, but a sociological critic; and the quality of his criticism will depend upon the quality of his understanding of the institutions and movements in present-day or past societies. For the sake of realism he must be in some degree an empiricist; he needs to distinguish between sociology and ideology, even while recognizing their relatedness; and he has a duty to resist being swept off his feet by every passing wind of ideology.

The present volume displays admirably some of these new directions in British sociology. The contributors examine a vital political problem. They do not transform it into a collection of trivial 'research topics', nor do they dismember it in order to distribute the parts in some abstract classificatory scheme; instead, they study it (on the basis of much useful research already carried out) in the relevant larger setting of colonialism, stratification, the economic system, and recent social movements such as Black Power, and they seek to connect the understanding of race and racialism with broader sociological theories. They analyse racialism as an ideology, and at the same time they are aware of the ideological commitments and personal values that sociologists themselves bring to the study of these questions. They criticize other conceptions and theories, and engage to some extent in controversy among themselves. The pattern they have established in this volume will, I am sure, affect profoundly the character of future conferences. We can expect to see, in the next few years, a concentration of attention upon issues of major social and political importance, more vigorous theoretical and ideological controversies, and a still larger incursion of sociologists into the public debate on long-term social aims and policies.

SAMI ZUBAIDA

Introduction[1]

The papers included in this volume were contributions to the BSA
Annual Conference, 1969, on the theme of Race Relations. The
intention of the conference organizers was to elicit contributions
that would discuss race relations in the context of 'mainstream'
sociology. In this way it was hoped that the conference would
contribute to the wider move on the part of some sociologists[2] to
integrate race relations into general sociological theory and discussion. Implicit in the organizers' intentions is a criticism of the
general field of race relations. This is obviously the place to state
and justify this criticism.

Sociological studies of race relations, with a few notable exceptions, have been a-theoretical and a-historical. They have also been
so excessively concerned with social problems that they have
tended to miss the sociological problems. They have tended to
study specific situations and to interpret them in an *ad hoc* fashion.
Few attempts were made to systematically relate specific situations
to the wider social structure. Such a systematic location of the
specific in the general context is a task that in sociology can best
be performed with the aid of theory. For it is one of the most
notable functions of theory in sociology, and one of the most
valuable contributions of the classical traditions of Durkheim,
Marx, and Weber, to present a picture of the totality of social
structure, showing the way in which different components of
structure are related together, and the way in which social groups
are located within this totality. Social groups can only be precisely
identified in terms of their relationships to other groups, and
the nature of such relationships is determined in part by the
systems of control over economic and political resources and

the associated systems of division of labour prevailing in that society.

The other set of determinants of group relations are to do with the systems of meanings, implicit and explicit, that contain knowledge and evaluation by the groups of one another. These ideological factors are not purely a function of the economic and political structures, but have a history of determinations in successive phases of the relationship between the groups in question. (It will be argued below, however, that these ideological systems are not logically consistent and rigid constructions, but are often contradictory and vague, suitable for a variety of usages to fit the specific situation.) To discuss social groups without undertaking the task of such analyses, or without relating to already existing analyses of such a nature, is to accept the prevailing social and ideological designations of the groups. This is in fact what most writers on race relations tend to do. The categories of 'race', 'colour', and 'ethnicity', although they refer to group characteristics that may be socially salient, are not necessarily adequate sociological designations. The situations of racial, ethnic, and migrant groups, of course, differ widely and qualitatively within each society, between societies, and at different historical periods. In other words 'race relations' are far from being homogeneous. What gives them their apparent homogeneity is their common definition as a social problem. The nature of the social problem, in turn, has been identified from 'liberal' and social-welfare perspectives. The major elements in such definitions are social psychological and micro-sociological, emphasizing prejudice and discrimination in interpersonal and community contexts. Studies with such an orientation may be valuable and interesting in that they give some descriptive insights into situations. However, because they do not concern themselves with the social-structural location of groups, they fail to distinguish between fundamentally different groups and situations, differences which, over time, crucially affect the nature of prejudice and discrimination. For example, in most American writings on race relations before the last few years, there is an implicit juxtaposition between Jews and Negroes in relation to the dominant European or American societies in which they live. They are both 'minority groups' against whom prejudice and discrimination operate. Their relations to other groups are 'race relations'. This preoccupation with the interpersonal processes in specific community-type contexts appears to preclude asking questions about the nature of the class and market positions and relationships to other groups and institutions in American society of Jews and Negroes respectively. Such considerations would conceptually reveal the vast differences between the two groups that we know to exist and that would account at least in part for the current confrontation between the two groups in New York. What obscured this obvious difference in previous writing is partly the social-psychological and micro-sociological orientation of research and discourse, and partly the definitions of *social* problems. It is no criticism of a field of study to say that it is concerned with social problems, but it *is* a criticism of that field to say that it defines its own sociological problems in accordance with the definition of social problems prevalent in that society. Thus, for a long time, race-relations research was primarily concerned with prejudice and discrimination, defined as problems by the 'liberal' agencies of the wider society. It is in part this perspective which results in obscuring the differences between Negroes and Jews. A macro-sociological, theoretically guided perspective would have to locate and define the groups in question in terms of their relationships to the wider social structure and the historical development of this relationship.

A historical dimension to the study and analysis of race relations is necessary for two reasons. One is to do with the fact that present group relations have a history and that many aspects of the present relationships can be better understood by relating them to their history. The second reason is that modern race-relations situations can be illuminated by comparison and juxtaposition with the wealth of historical examples of group relations of the type designated 'race relations' in the modern context. A neglect of these examples often leads to a narrow ethnocentrism and simplistic 'common-sense' interpretations.

It is becoming increasingly clear that the historical legacy of colonialism enters in important ways into shaping relationships between black or 'coloured' minorities and white majorities in Europe and the US. Phases in the development of Western capitalism gave rise to different types of relationship with the colonial peoples: early conquest and trading relationships accompanied and closely followed by enslavement and the extensive use of slave labour in production of raw materials; British colonial administration and military presence in many areas of the colonial world for over a century; and finally with the need for labour after the Second World War for industrial expansion in Britain, the importation of labour from ex-colonial territories, leading to the present 'immigrant problem'. We can see from this perspective how the situation in which the 'coloured' ex-colonial groups are inferior and underprivileged is created by the historical development of capitalism and colonialism. It is also the economic situation of the post-colonial world that determines the patterns and conditions of labour migration. A most important aspect of this development are the cognitive structures that shape conceptions of inferiority and superiority. These cognitive structures (beliefs, stereotype, and 'common-sense' knowledge) in terms of which people in Britain experience coloured minorities must be profoundly imbued with accumulations of colonial experience. The beliefs and stereotypes acquired and disseminated by generations of working-class soldiers and middle-class administrators in the colonies are available to our contemporaries. Many of these cognitions are derogatory, some are patronizing, a few are favourable, but there is one theme underlying all of them: the inferiority and servility of 'native' populations. In this respect, immigrant communities from the ex-colonies are not entirely new to the British people. At times when the economic and political conditions are conducive to increased tensions between the communities, the more negative elements of these cognitions are aroused and modified to fit the current themes.

The other reason for stressing the importance of historical study is the great wealth of examples of group relations in different stratification systems that history offers us. By contrasting one social structure to other relevant structures, it is possible to increase the 'visibility' of processes within it. Further, processes of social–structural change can only be seen when looking at societies over time. Those sociologists who forgo historical comparisons tend to become so centred within present society as to interpret the phenomena they are investigating in the terms of that society. Consider, for instance, the explanation advanced by some writers[3] of the attitudes to coloured immigrants in Britain in terms of the cultural strangeness of these groups. At a 'common-sense' level such an explanation was appealing at a time when the more virulent forms of racial prejudice and discrimination were still dormant. However, the inadequacy of such an explanation becomes apparent when viewed in a historical and comparative context. We have many historical examples of 'strangers' intruding into host societies, some as conquerors, some as slaves, some as itinerant merchants, and some as indentured labourers. The resulting patterns of group relations and attitudes were, of course, highly variable depending on the nature of these 'strangers' and the way in which they related to that society. Seen in this perspective the category of 'strangeness' in itself does not explain anything. Such a conclusion would also direct attention to the nature of these strangers – immigrant labourers from poor and dependent ex-colonies – and raise problems for research on the ways in which such workers were being integrated[4] into the systems of power and stratification in British society.

It can be argued, with justification, that many of the criticisms levelled here at the field of race relations can also be applied to much empirical research in other fields of sociology. Indeed, most sociological research in Britain and the US has been a-theoretical and a-historical. However, in this respect, one particular aspect that distinguishes the field is that it has been largely neglected by the few sociologists who were working with theoretical and historical perspectives. The reasons for this neglect and some of its consequences are discussed in David Lockwood's contribution to this volume.

Some of the themes raised so far in this introductory essay are relevant, in various contexts, to the other contributions. Let us now move to a consideration of these contributions. The aim here will be to consider the main arguments presented by the authors with the object of posing some of the problems that follow from them.

Both David Lockwood and John Rex in their papers attempt to bring race relations into the mainstream of the classic tradition in sociology. The questions they both ask are about the nature of group relationships involved in 'race relations' and how they relate to the more general stratification systems and the social structures of which they are a part. Rex's contribution is valuable in that it presents a classification of race-relations situations in terms of the nature of the power relationships between the groups and the function each group has for the other. This classification takes into account the heterogeneity of race-relations situations. But given such a variety, what can be the focus of a sociology of race relations? Rex answers this question as follows:

'[The sociology of race relations] is concerned with a broad range of stratification situations (using this term in a wide sense to include any situation in which power and privilege are un-equally distributed between groups or individual role-players in a social structure), but only in so far as roles or group member-ships are ascribed in terms of observable physical or cultural characteristics such as those which distinguish groups of colonial conquerors and conquered and only if the system as a whole is justified by deterministic beliefs' (p. 50, below).

This identification, however, does raise an important question of which Rex is well aware. The question is: under what conditions do such 'deterministic' or racialist ideologies develop? While ascriptive definitions and allocations are common in most human societies, ascription on the basis of 'physical and cultural charac-teristics' prescribed by deterministic beliefs is specific to particular situations in particular societies. Belief systems and definitions of this type cannot be assumed to be random, but have to be explained in terms of the social structures in which they arise. Rex, while clearly recognizing this problem, does not give any clear indica-tions of the kind of factors that can illuminate it. He does suggest that the dominant ideological/religious system in a society can play an important causal role in determining whether racialist ideologies arise in that society. It will be argued below that there are certain difficulties involved in this approach. For the moment let us emphasize that, quite apart from the origin and development of racialist ideologies, once they are *institutionalized* into governmental, legal, and economic practices, they become primary factors in the stratification systems of which they form a part. That is, the race-relations situation is not just stratification plus racialist ideology and ascription, but the very dynamics of the stratification system become profoundly influenced by its racial elements. Witness the situation in the US. On this point we are fully in agreement with Rex.

The main question Lockwood is asking is whether race relations can be described and analysed in terms of the concepts and propositions of general sociology or whether any special concepts are needed to deal with them. In particular he is concerned with the question of whether patterns of racial superiority/inferiority conform to the Marxian paradigm of class domination, conflict, and revolution. He considers notions of 'plural society', particularly as elaborated by Van den Berghe (1967), and analyses their relationship to the Marxian paradigm. The interest of these notions is that they have developed specifically from the study of race-relations situations, and if they can be subsumed under the rubric of general class theories then we can conclude that no special terms are needed for the analysis of race relations. However, Lockwood concludes that they cannot be so subsumed. Whereas the Marxian paradigm and its derivations are concerned with internally developed stratification, notions of 'plural society' refer to stratification situations brought about by exogenous factors such as conquest and migration. Even when the lines of division between racial groups coincide with class lines, the *consciousness* of the conflict is in terms of race and not class, and the object of the struggle is not so much to change the system in the Marxian sense of 'revolution', but to reverse the relationship of domination between the groups, or at least to challenge the dominance of the superior group. We can agree with Lockwood that stratification situations in which race is an important element are different in certain respects from stratification situations not involving such elements. Some important points, however, must be made explicit in relation to his argument. The first is that 'pluralist' situations are far from being homogeneous: the great difference between Jews and 'coloured' groups in their relations to the dominant society have already been argued. If we consider the great variety of situations to be found in different historical settings the heterogeneity becomes even more bewildering. Consider, for instance, the great structural differences between the following relationships: military slaves of diverse origins in Islamic empires to their masters and to the subject populations; 'barbaric' conquerors to the settled 'civilized' populations; master–slave relations in slave plantations; 'immigrant–host' relations in contemporary Britain. All these can be classified as 'pluralist' situations and yet there is no theory of plural societies that explains variations within the category. 'Plural society' is a very general descriptive term. On the other hand, these variations *can* be explained in terms of general sociological theories of power structures, economic structures, and patterns of stratification associated with them. For plural societies do clearly constitute systems of production and domination to which the groups are differentially related. The groups that migrate into a particular society soon become integrated into the indigenous systems of production and domination: conquerors proceed to dominate and exploit, slaves are only transported for their labour power, migrant workers are assigned to particular kinds of work which native workers would not do, and so on. This is *not* to say that they necessarily become integrated into existing native classes. It is clear, for instance, that immigrant workers in this country do not share similar market positions with the native workers. Their relationships to the trade unions, political parties, local government, and the state are also clearly different from that of native workers. These differences are the main components of 'race relations', and a consideration of such differences is essential for the understanding of other aspects of the relationships between the groups. Lockwood would, perhaps, not disagree with the points made here. His main concern is to show how the focus of conflict is necessarily different in a plural society from that in an indigenous class society. The implication of the argument presented here, however, is that patterns of consciousness, conflict, and struggle will vary with the development of the general stratification system and the economic and political structures. The rapid development of militant black consciousness in the US from exclusivist Black Power movement to a combination of this with a more general revolutionary consciousness shows the difficulty of maintaining a necessarily permanent distinction between the two forms of conflict.

Of the empirical contributions to this volume, Sheila Allen's and Harold Wolpe's, though concerned with different problems, have in common an explicit commitment to the study of race-relations situations and problems as aspects of the more general social structures. Allen's paper reports on research into relationships between Pakistani workers in Bradford and trade unions. She attempts to see race or ethnicity as an aspect of the general employment and trade-union situation in the city rather than as a problem in itself. What is particularly interesting about this contribution is that it shows how problems of trade-union recruitment and organization, commonly attributed to the facts of ethnic differences, are really more general problems of the type of industry and employment situation. Further, the attribution of problems to ethnic differences by trade-union officials and to racial discrimination by the immigrant workers may result in the separate organization of immigrant workers in order to protect their interests in the light of the perceived failure of trade unions to do so. Thus it appears that the labelling of general problems as 'racial' may bring about the emergence of specifically racial situations.

Wolpe, in his paper, discusses racial stratification in South Africa in relation to economic developments in that country. In particular, he examines the thesis, put forward by a number of students of South African society, asserting the incompatibility between the 'logic' of industrialism and the policies of apartheid. The implication of this thesis is that racialist policies originating in the political and ideological spheres are imposed on an economy that can be more efficiently managed without racial discrimination. Wolpe criticizes this thesis and goes on to show how racial discrimination was highly functional for the development of South

African mining, industry, and farming. It may be argued, however, that as industry becomes capital-intensive, the importance of cheap labour declines and the easy availability of skills becomes crucial. The availability of skills, it is contended, is severely curtailed by a system that limits educational and training opportunities to the white minority. Even though Wolpe does not argue explicitly against such a thesis, it is possible to counter it from the evidence he presents. He shows that South African industrial management has used considerable flexibility in the classification of skills to suit labour demands. Whenever there is a shortage of a particular skill formerly reserved for white workers, black labour is trained for and drafted into the appropriate occupational category at suitably lower wages. The Bantu Education Act, in securing literacy and some degree of education to a substantial proportion of black children, facilitates this flexibility in classification of skills by providing a background for further training. It does not appear from this that apartheid policies are inconsistent with economic efficiency.

Wolpe's contribution is particularly interesting in relation to the 'plural society' arguments we have just discussed. It shows that plural societies like South Africa, while empirically different from ethnically homogeneous societies, are best analysed in terms of the general sociological categories pertaining to power structures and stratification systems.

John Lambert, in his paper, discusses some of the problems involved in relationships between immigrants and police. He argues that traditional police definitions and perceptions of types of 'client' are difficult to apply to immigrants and their situations. In the resulting uncertainty, the policeman tends to fall back on his 'citizen attitudes', which consist largely of derogatory stereotypes of coloured immigrants. Characteristic immigrant responses to police, sometimes also based on inaccurate expectations, tend to aggravate the policeman's stereotypes. Lambert's arguments make certain assumptions about the prevalence of a working consensus among the native population on the policeman's function and authority. Such assumptions may be justified, especially within particular spheres of police operation. There are certain apparent developments in Britain, however, which may have repercussions on police–public relations with particular consequences for police–immigrant relations. The increasing direct-action militancy of a number of diverse groups in Britain is being defined as a 'law-and-order problem'. There are increasing pressures on government and local authorities to take firm action against such developments. At the time of writing, the Conservative Shadow Cabinet had just announced its intention to introduce legislation increasing police and court powers to deal with such offenders. The consequence of such governmental action is likely to be an increase in police confrontation with various, usually articulate, groups of citizens. We have already witnessed such confrontations and the accompanying volume of complaints against police action by certain sections of the public and the press. The involvement of immigrant groups in the 'Civil Rights' type of issue is likely to increase their representation in the ranks of protesting citizens. The kinds of process described by Lambert may in such situations result in the singling-out and scapegoating of immigrant groups. Such measures may be in tune with certain popular sentiments resulting from the increasing salience of 'race-relations problems'. If such processes do occur, which is not un-likely, they may well result in a transformation in police–public and police–immigrant relationships into patterns in which overt conflict becomes an increasingly prominent feature. In order to take account of such developments, police relationships to various sectors of the public are perhaps best studied in the context of local and national power structures.

Nicholas Deakin's contribution is valuable in that it exposes the vacuity of certain assumptions about the illiberality of public opinion that have been the stock-in-trade of some politicians in recent years. Further consideration of this contribution should perhaps be reserved for the general discussion of the question of ideology. It is to this discussion that we shall now turn.

The question of ideology features prominently in some of the contributions to this volume. John Rex is inclined to attach a great deal of significance to dominant ideologies in determining patterns of race relations; on p. 51, for instance, he states:

'Of some importance with regard to the development of stratification situations in a racialist direction is the sort of religious or political ideology that is available. Thus it does seem to be the case that race looms less large as a problem in Catholic countries because Catholic social teaching is inhospitable to the notion of deterministic differences between men, and in this may be contrasted with Calvinism, which contains within itself the deterministic distinction between the elect and the damned.'

The problem of ideology is a thorny one. It is very difficult to make general statements about the functions of ideology in social structure. Ideologies have different functions in different configurations of social structures, and in different situations within the same society. Moreover, the degree of consistency and rigidity of ideological structure is highly variable. To take obviously contrasting examples, the functions of Puritan ideology in Calvinist Geneva are clearly different from those of Catholic ideology in relation to natives and slaves in colonial South America. In the former case a whole civic community is consciously and rigidly organized in accordance with a religious system. In the latter, a wider range of flexible and sometimes contradictory interpretations is open to people acting in different situations with different interests. Indeed, flexibility of interpretation and adaptability to different situations seem to be characteristic of most ideological structures. Consistency and rigidity of ideology and its conscious involvement in the close regulation of action appear to be features of 'charismatic' or revolutionary communities and situations. However, because dominant ideological systems have important *cognitive* functions in that they provide the categories of thought that shape experience, it can be argued that they can inhibit certain types of thinking and facilitate others. But with a world religion like Christianity it is difficult to argue such unitary influences. Its branches, whether Orthodox, Catholic, or Protestant, have been moulded in such a variety of social settings over such long periods of history that they all contain a multiplicity of cognitive and evaluative strands that can be drawn upon for various purposes. In the field of race relations, this is demonstrated by the great variety of conflicting Christian rulings and interpretations on the subject in the past as well as in the present day. In this, Catholic societies have not been noted for any greater uniformity of interpretation, nor for greater liberalism in the treatment of their subject peoples.

Our own times, while clearly not marked by the end of ideology, hopefully predicted by some American sociologists during the last decade, *are* characterized by a fragmentation of ideology. The loss of innocence we have suffered over the last century makes it difficult for us to sustain any one of the great ideological systems of the eighteenth and nineteenth centuries in its entirety. Elements of *laissez-faire* and utilitarian ideologies, of Marxism and other socialist thought, of organismic and statist doctrines, of the various strands of Christian thought as well as elements of scientific thought: all these are available to people in modern society to draw upon in the formulation of their experiences and of their attitudes to issues and events. Not even members of the most sectarian political groups can avoid implicit participation in radically opposite thought systems. However, it is likely that different groups in the population participate differentially in these ideologies; it is not unreasonable to suppose, for instance, that intellectual and professional strata would show greater consistency in their eclecticism.

This point has a direct bearing on Michael Banton's contribution to this volume. Banton, quite rightly, points out that the pronouncements of the leading segregationist and anti-immigrant spokesmen in this country do not draw upon biological theories of racial superiority/inferiority, but on sociological, psychological, and ethnological findings. He argues, on the ground of the historical development of the doctrine, that 'racism' should be confined to its reference to the biological theories and that to use the term in the present context is to do no more than to label people and ideas we do not like with a gratifying epithet. In the interests of accuracy and rigour, we should distinguish between 'racist' biologically based doctrines and modern segregationist or illiberal ideologies and practices. Quite apart from what label is to be used, the shift in the basis of segregationist ideologies is obviously important and of considerable sociological interest. However, in his argument Banton is in danger of attributing unitary and consistent ideological outlooks to the segregationist groups. While it is true to say that public spokesmen such as Enoch Powell and Peter Griffiths no longer resort to biological doctrines, it is doubtful whether their new ideological orientations are shared by the mass of their non-intellectual followers. In the absence of empirical studies on the subject, one can only make guesses on the basis of impressions. A study of the correspondence columns of provincial newspapers, for instance, will show quite clearly that biological doctrines are still very much alive among certain sections of the population.

Banton's historical account of the development of biological notions and theories of race is also of interest in a discussion of ideology. He argues that scientific theories of race are best understood in the context of the *scientific* problems and assumptions prevalent at the time. The tendency among modern liberal writers to see them as ideology, prejudice, and error is based on a questionable approach to the history of science that involves 'grading' past scientific theories in accordance with their truth value in the light of our present knowledge and in relation to their political and ideological implications for our present social problems. These are gratifying criticisms of the textbook approach to the history of science and the naïve realism prevalent among certain writers on the subject. It should be a prime methodological principle for all sociologists and historians of ideas that items under study should first be related to the structures of which they are part and understood in the context of such structures. While many scholars will pay lip-service to this principle, few of them, alas, employ it in practice. However, to proclaim the scientific nature of a theory is not to exempt it from analysis as an ideology. It is perfectly legitimate to consider any theory from two perspectives: as a scientific theory and as an ideology. In the first perspective we are concerned with its validity and its relationship to the body of science of which it forms a part. In the second we are concerned with its ideological functions for social groups and their interests. As social scientists we should be well aware of this duality of perspectives, for this is often the procedure we follow with our own theories, whether implicitly or explicitly. Banton's contention that the imputation of ideological function does not explain the *origin* of biological theories of race is probably correct. Nor does such imputation necessarily explain the motives of the scientists in question. However, to argue that such theories had ideological functions at that time and subsequently is not necessarily to imply that these functions explain the origin of the theories, nor is it necessary to contend that their authors were themselves racist ideologues. The appeal of these theories to racist thinkers, their elaboration to justify European domination, and their subsequent persistence, surely all combine to show their importance as ideological weapons.

Deakin's contribution is also relevant to the question of ideology. In the main part of his paper he reports on a study of the attitudes of 'opinion leaders' in Wolverhampton and their perceptions of the degree of agreement of public opinion in general with their view. The findings are interesting in that they show how leaders assume a much greater degree of illiberality among their followers than is actually the case. The potentialities of this kind of investigation are of great interest for the study of political ideologies. It may be possible, for instance, to trace the processes of reciprocal shaping of ideology among the leaders and their followers and the way in which ideologies, institutionalized in political parties, are shifted in accordance with situational pressures. However, the use of conventional questionnaire methods of attitude study does have some serious limitations. Given the fragmentation and situational relativity of ideology noted above, it is difficult to know which fragment is being elicited in the questionnaire or interview situation, and how reliable an indication it is of the ideological configurations in the respondents' cognitive repertories.

Deakin's respondents appear very much in the role of the liberal apologist, accounting to a more liberal outsider for the illiberality of opinion and practice they assume to exist in their areas. These responses are not very reliable indications of what ideology, or fragments of ideologies, these same persons would adopt in different situations under different pressures. Observational or documentary studies of the positions adopted by 'leaders' in relation to various situations would tell us a great deal more about the processes of opinion formation and propagation. This is, of course, one of the regular dilemmas of sociological research: between the accessible and systematic questionnaire study with little information yield on social structure and process and the more difficult and often inaccessible observational and documentary study.

In this Introduction, issues were raised that were judged to be of general sociological importance. Some of these issues are pursued in more specific contexts in the contributions to follow.

Notes

1 I wish to thank Mary McIntosh for her comments on an earlier draft of this essay.
2 After the early pioneering effort of Oliver Cromwell Cox (1948) in this direction, some more recent workers have undertaken this task. See, for instance, Van den Berghe (1967), Banton (1967), Glass (1964), and Rex and Moore (1967).
3 See, for instance, Patterson (1963); Banton (1967: 368–84) makes limited use of this hypothesis.
4 The term 'integrated' is being used here in the sense of fitting into a stratification hierarchy and a system of division of labour *not* in the sense of 'assimilation'. In this sense it can be said, for example, that slaves were integrated into the plantation system of production.

References

BANTON, MICHAEL 1967. *Race Relations.* London: Tavistock Publications; New York: Basic Books.
COX, OLIVER CROMWELL 1948. *Caste, Class and Race: a study in social dynamics.* New York: Doubleday.
GLASS, RUTH 1964. Insiders–Outsiders, the position of minorities. Transactions of 5th World Congress of Sociology 1962, Vol. III, Louvain, I.S.A. 1964.
PATTERSON, SHEILA 1963. *Dark Strangers.* London: Tavistock; Bloomington: Indiana University Press.
REX, JOHN, & MOORE, ROBERT 1967. *Race, Community and Conflict.* London: Oxford University Press.
VAN DEN BERGHE, PIERRE L. 1967. *Race and Racism.* New York: Wiley.

MICHAEL BANTON

The Concept of Racism

If one seeks to reduce intolerance towards ethnic minorities, the first essential is a correct diagnosis. The importance of this is not always appreciated because of the moral indignation that discrimination evokes and the reluctance of activists to accept any delay. But mistakes are sometimes made that cause anti-discrimination campaigns to be fruitless or even to exacerbate the situation. For example, some groups have thought that if, by conducting a survey, they were to expose the prevalence of discrimination, this would shock people into taking or supporting remedial action. Frequently it has the reverse effect. Those who discriminate derive support from learning that so many others do so too. The authorities may take fright and decline to act against what they see as a powerful section of the population.

In considering the diagnostic value of the concept of racism, we need to start with a definition. The word is a relatively new one and it is employed in different senses. One of the first writers to make extended use of it was Ruth Benedict in a book that in its London edition was given the title *Race and Racism* (1940). She comes nearest to a definition when she writes that 'racism is the dogma that one ethnic group is condemned by nature to congenital inferiority and another group is destined to congenital superiority'. Social scientists have, in general, followed this lead in viewing racism as essentially a doctrine. The kernel of this doctrine is found in the assertions: (*a*) that people's culture and psychological characteristics are genetically determined; and (*b*) that the genetic determinants are grouped in patterns that can be identified with human races in the old morphological sense that envisaged the existence of pure races. Grouping these features, I have defined

17

racism as the doctrine that a man's behaviour is determined by stable inherited characters deriving from separate racial stocks having distinctive attributes and usually considered to stand to one another in relations of superiority and inferiority.

Several standard textbooks of race relations and sociological reference works do not define racism. Those authorities who do define it do not differ substantially from the viewpoint I have set out. Shibutani and Kwan speak of racism as an ideology; Van den Berghe calls it a set of beliefs, saying 'only when group differences in physical traits are considered a determinant of social behaviour and moral or intellectual qualities can we properly speak of racism'. Webster's *Dictionary* calls it an assumption of the same character. The Gould and Kolb *Dictionary of the Social Sciences* (1964) calls racism 'the doctrine that there is a connection between racial and cultural traits'.

Of particular interest is Margaret Nicholson's *Dictionary of American-English Usage* (1957) which under the entry 'racialism, racism' states: 'If there is differentiation, *racism* is more often applied to the doctrine, *racialism* to the practice of the doctrine.' Another relevant distinction is that which Harris draws when he contrasts 'scientific racism' with 'folk racism, a popular system of prejudice and discrimination directed against one endogamous descent group by another [which] is probably as old as humanity' (Harris, 1968: 81). Yet once the identification of racism as a doctrine is stretched to cover folk beliefs, or, in modified form to denote practices that are not consequences of the doctrine, a major difficulty arises. I am not persuaded that it is proper to speak of race-consciousness or racism in times or places where people do not employ a concept of race. The sentiments Romans felt towards Celts, for example, are indicative of ethnocentrism and of antipathy towards certain kinds of strangers, but there is no warrant for calling them racial. Group hostilities can have many causes and the presence of what we now recognize as racial differences between two parties does not necessarily give these hostilities a special character.

However we define racism we have to contend with its pejorative connotation. It is not a neutral word. It has been said that in the social sciences our concepts tend to become epithets, but Everett Hughes remarks that in sociology many of our concepts were epithets before we took them up. He writes 'a considerable part of sociology consists of cleaning up the language in which common people talk of social and moral problems. We make great efforts to make bad things better by change of name, and we try, too, to make things disappear by giving them bad names. This used to be called exorcism' (1952: 131). Racism is at present both a concept and an epithet. We cannot prevent its being an epithet but if, as sociologists, we wish to use it for diagnostic purposes, then we should try to use it in a systematic manner. I shall contend that our desire to use it as an epithet has muddied its use as a concept and may therefore have supported an error in diagnosis that hampers the campaign against intolerance.

THE ORIGINS OF RACISM

If we are to use racism as a concept we ought to try to identify the first expression of the doctrine and to determine when and how it got started. The first book to set out a systematic doctrine of racism was Knox's *The Races of Men* in 1850. Gobineau's *Essai* was published in Paris in 1853. Nott and Gliddon's *Types of Mankind* appeared in the following year from American and English publishers. The nearly simultaneous and independent publication of these treatises in three different countries is quite striking. The coincidence of their publication with the demise of slavery is also notable, for it can be argued that, as slavery was abolished, some people sought new justifications for maintaining the subordination of those who had earlier been exploited by being counted as property.

From a historical standpoint, racism was an outgrowth of the morphological approach to human biology associated with the study of comparative anatomy. This was a static, non-evolutionary view of human characteristics that made no allowance for natural selection. Its limitations did not become fully apparent (and then only gradually) until after 1900 when Mendel's work was rediscovered and the outlines of the genetic system were mapped. The

B

first statement of the approach that was to beget racism came, appropriately, from the great anatomist Cuvier in the chronologically convenient year of 1800 (Hocking, 1968: 29–31). Throughout the second half of the century racism was a doctrine with serious, if somewhat outlandish, scientific pretensions. For a while it seemed as if a Mark Two racism was supported by Darwin's work, and the early studies in genetics could be interpreted in similar vein. Racism, then, contained an element of science which was crucial to its success. But this was not all. The idea that the Saxon peoples might be biologically superior to Celts and Slavs, and white races to black, was seized upon, magnified, and publicized, because it was convenient to those who held power in the Europe of that day. Europeans were flattered when told that they were innately superior. The possibility of a biological explanation of cultural differences was therefore entertained more sympathetically than the evidence warranted. So two other elements in the success of racism were its political utilization and the inability of some of its exponents to assess the evidence in an objective manner. Some recent writers have been so impressed by these two elements that they have neglected the scientific component and their interpretations of the history of racism have been misleading. Three kinds of explanation can be distinguished:

(i) racist theories appeared as a scientific response to the ideological needs of contemporary capitalism;
(ii) racist theories originated in the racial prejudices of their authors;
(iii) racist theories originated in scientific mistakes.

It should be emphasized that these are kinds of explanation, whereas the arguments advanced by particular authors often employ a combination of two or three of them.

Anthony MARX

THE FUNCTIONAL EXPLANATION

The first kind of explanation employs a functional model of the social system. It has been developed primarily by writers heavily influenced by Marxism. This approach to sociological reasoning

is, of course, in many respects sharply opposed to functionalism.
But when trying to account for racism many Marxist writers do
make use of one variety of functional explanation. Foremost
among them is Oliver Cromwell Cox, who defined 'race prejudice'
in terms very close to the contemporary meaning of racism. For
him, it was 'a social attitude propagated among the public by an
exploiting class for the purpose of stigmatizing some group as
inferior, so that the exploitation of either the group itself or its
resources or both may be justified'. There is a suggestion here that
once the student has understood that racism is a cover for exploitation that is enough. It only remains for him to trace out the way
in which its socio-political function moulds its form of expression.
Determining function is all-important. Cox argues that racism is
not to be confused with anti-Semitism. They are different because
their political functions are different.

While recognizing that racism may have such functions, I have
argued that racial hostility has other aspects too, and that it is
also a psychological, sociological, geographical, historical phenomenon and much else besides. I have maintained that these other
aspects need to be studied in their own right. This is where the
divergence between Marxists and non-Marxists starts. A historian
who has developed a Marxist analysis of race relations in Latin
America picks me up on this point. He writes, 'Economic, social
and political phenomena are always geographically determined,
and these conditions as a complex reality, are psychologically
summarized in or managed by racism, as in and by many other
psychological entities, so as to serve the purpose of the realization
and maintenance of the respective economic or social conditions'
(Lipschutz 1969: 205). The difference between us is the familiar
one of a distinction between the elaboration of a theory and the
utilization of a particular kind of model. Most contemporary
social scientists understand by theory a structure of interrelated
hypotheses which can be extended by testing and falsification. In
this process comparison is vital. It is essential to identify the
common elements in the prejudice shown towards Jews, Negroes,
and Catholics in order to improve our understanding of prejudice
and improve the structure of hypotheses. Marxists are unwilling

to formulate propositions which they would accept as falsifiable, which shows that they use the word 'theory' in a different sense. They operate with a model of society that offers guidelines for the analysis of how power is used in societies; this model can be applied most fruitfully to the study of the historical sequence of events in a particular society or in several interrelated societies. The principal objection that non-Marxist sociologists make against the Marxist representation of racism as a passive element used to realize political goals is the implication that racism is caused by its consequence. Nothing can be caused by its consequence. The functions of racism do not account for its origin.

THE INDUCTIVIST EXPLANATION

The second kind of explanation is chiefly found in the writings of American sociologists. They are acquainted with racism in its modern forms and work backwards, viewing earlier statements about race from a modern standpoint instead of setting them in the intellectual context of the time in which they were made. They take it for granted that doctrines of racial superiority are unjustified and wonder how it can be that earlier writers did not see this. They infer that they must have been biased or themselves inclined to prejudice. This way of writing the history of science has been examined by Joseph Agassi, who calls it an application of the inductive philosophy of science. This is a more developed version of what Butterfield called the whig view of history. The inductivist historian starts from the modern textbook and shows how it was constructed, giving plus marks to the scientists whose theories have been accepted and minus marks for unsuccessful work. Sometimes, of course, an old theory is found to be better than it was thought, and in a new edition of the history book the plus and minus marks have to be readjusted.

David Hume, in a footnote to his essay *Of National Characters* (1748), noted that alone among the races of the world the Negro race has never developed any major civilization. On this account he suspected that Negroes might be naturally inferior to the whites. A contemporary American commentator's interpretation is that

Hume 'echoed the belief in white supremacy accepted by most of his compatriots' (Rose 1968: 18). Hume's judgement is not as simple-minded as it may appear, and indeed his views on the differences between peoples might well repay much closer study (cf. McPhee 1968: 525). Nor are there good grounds for so positive a statement about the beliefs of his contemporaries. The idea of white supremacy is a more modern one, which cannot be read back into an earlier period without giving a false impression. Another modern writer (Hirsch 1968: 38) refers to the 1866 paper in which Langdon Down for the first time identified and named the variety of mental defect now called Down's syndrome or mongolism. Down thought that such children were a reversion to the Mongoloid racial type. Our contemporary cites this as an example of the racial hierarchy theory and of a *pattern of thinking* that has persisted for one hundred years. This judgement is made in ignorance of what scientists thought about race in the 1860s. In explaining the mistake as the outcome of Down's pattern of think-ing, the critic neatly exemplifies the inductivist theory of error as the product of bias that was so precisely stated by Bacon. For another example, there is a much respected textbook of American race relations that discusses the nineteenth-century theories about race that we now know to be mistaken as examples of the 'mystical' view of race (Simpson and Yinger 1965: 27). This surely implies that the theories were wrong because their authors adopted the wrong outlook, instead of locating the errors within a historical pattern of discovery. The next generation will discover error in what many modern pundits believe to be truth. Perhaps they will explain away our mistakes as the product of our prejudices.

Some writers on the history of racial thought employ an in-ductivist approach without ever committing themselves to it. For example, an American historian presents a series of quotations from writers who espoused ideas of racial superiority without considering why men of their generation could not attain the understanding of later decades. He presents racism as 'a dogma of Western pseudo-science . . . the product of the anxieties of the age – brought on by rapid political and socio-economic changes'. He writes, 'Racialists, not satisfied with merely proclaiming the superiority of the white over the coloured race, also felt it necessary to erect a hierarchy within the white race itself' (Snyder 1962: 98–9, 39). This implies that they could have avoided error had they only sought the truth conscientiously, so that racism was the product of a pseudo-scientific conspiracy.

Others have written, at times at considerable length, on the history of ideas concerning race without ever trying to explain what it is that differentiates modern racism from expressions of racial hostility in antiquity. They are ready to stigmatize some earlier writers as racists without defining the term. For example, 'Many a racist awaited breathlessly some scheme of race classification that would withstand the testing methods of science . . . how little the search really mattered may be seen in the tendency of racists, when a physical basis of measurable race differences eluded them, to assume immense innate psychological differences in any case' (Gossett 1963: 82–3). This, I would claim, is implicitly inductivist, though the tendency of such authors to avoid developing any clear explanations of the evidence they amass is exasperating.

RACISM AS A SCIENTIFIC MISTAKE

The third kind of explanation pictures racist theories as conjectural explanations of problems as they appear to scientists and scholars of the contemporary age. For example, one authority describes Gobineau's identification of race with culture as 'an honest intellectual error' (Lévi-Strauss 1952: 5). Later on, new evidence may refute these conjectures. If people persist in clinging to hypotheses in the face of overwhelmingly contrary evidence they may then be suspected of bias or prejudice. This approach locates the origin of racism within the history of science.

Some would say that this is not the right place for it. One of the first historians of racial ideas was Théophile Simar, who in 1922 published an *Étude critique sur la formation de la doctrine des races au XVIIIᵉ siècle et son expansion au XIXᵉ siècle*. He maintained that, though theories of race claim to be based on discoveries in anthropology, in fact they owe nothing to it and arose outside anthropology. Simar says that the doctrine of race was originally one of class superiority associated with the claims of the French nobility and the criticism of the Revolution. It was an outgrowth of the romantic philosophy and the Protestant doctrine of predestination which was used to attack Latin civilization and the papacy. Racism certainly has roots in eighteenth- and nineteenth-century philosophy of history but I would not accept the contention that its growth was independent of developments in anthropology. Had the historians and philosophers who elaborated such ideas been pressed about them, they would have fallen back upon anthropological hypotheses. The anthropology of that time was also more committed to racial ideas than Simar realized.

In terms of the definition I advanced earlier, the first racist was Robert Knox, the Edinburgh anatomist who suffered public obloquy, probably unfairly, because of his association with Burke and Hare. They were men who murdered several defenceless persons to sell their bodies for dissection in the medical school. Knox lived from 1791 to 1862. He had his precursors, of course, but this is only to be expected. Knox linked his explanations of biological variation to cultural differences, describing his theory as 'transcendental anatomy'. In Knox's hierarchy the Slav and Gothic races were ranked *above* the Saxon and Celt, but notions of superiority were not important to Knox. He held that each race was adapted to one habitat. Europeans could never succeed in colonizing the tropics, they could not even acclimatize themselves to life in America, for the continent belonged to the Indians. Knox followed Cuvier, his greatly respected Parisian teacher, in identifying the racial differences in which anatomists were beginning to interest themselves with cultural differences. He made a mistake. It seems probable that the blight that had been cast on his own career introduced into his teaching about race a bitter extravagance and made it difficult for him to adopt a judicious approach to the mass of conflicting and often unreliable evidence about race available to a scientist of his generation. But if he had not made this mistake someone else would probably have done.

At the beginning of the nineteenth century many scientists interested in the field believed that all men were the descendants of Adam and Eve. Few entertained seriously the suggestion that mankind consisted of different species. The idea of a 'great chain of being' which had been so powerful in late eighteenth-century biology tended to deny specific differences of any kind at all. This in part explains the approach of the Manchester surgeon Charles White, who in 1799 published *An Account of the Regular Gradation in Man, and in different Animals and Vegetables; and from the former to the latter.* He measured anatomical features of over fifty Negroes and compared them with measurements for whites, claiming that they fitted this pattern of gradation from vegetables through the animal kingdom up through the primates to the Europeans. White insisted that he wished to see the pernicious practice of enslaving humans everywhere abolished, but this had not prevented his being pilloried as a racist by later writers.

Another facet of the contemporary Biblical anthropology was the belief that the world was no more than seven thousand years old. According to Archbishop Ussher's computation, 'the beginning of time fell upon the night before the twenty-third of October in the year of the Julian Calendar 710'. Other calculations estimated the creation not in 4004 B.C. but in 3928, 4146, or 5411 B.C. If, as anthropologists then believed, the kinds of man had developed from an original, possibly dark-skinned, ancestor over so short a period, the physical constitution of mankind must be capable of quite rapid change. Why there should be different races was difficult to explain. If scientists could solve the puzzle, they might in so doing find a key to human history. Interpretation of the evidence might be influenced by religious belief, but from a scientific standpoint there was no *a priori* reason why race and culture might not be causally related. The proposition that race determined culture was at this time a reasonable if highly speculative hypothesis. No one can say the same thing today.

To appreciate Langdon Down's characterization of a form of mental defect as a reversion to the Mongoloid racial type, it is essential to grasp the contemporary belief in the possibility of fairly rapid physical changes. Many men were afraid that European racial attributes could be subject to speedy degeneration. It is important also to understand that the development hypothesis took forms that now seem strange. According to a theory in contemporary embryology, ontogeny recapitulated phylogeny. A man became a man only by passing through transitional stages of organization in which he was first similar to the embryonic forms of fishes, reptiles, birds, and mammals before attaining human form (Glass 1959: 309, 373, 409–10, 440, 457). The application of this line of reasoning to differences within the human species was only to be expected. In the highly influential book *Vestiges of Creation* (1843), it is asserted that 'the leading characters of the various races of mankind are simply representations of particular stages in the development of the highest or Caucasian type . . . The Mongolian is an arrested infant newly born'. The Chinese were said to be a child race. Down's theory that, while many of the patients in his mental hospital were Caucasian, others resembled the Ethiopian, Malay, and Mongolian racial types, reversions to earlier developmental forms, was in the context of 1866 an interesting idea. Because it is derogatory to non-Europeans and because we now believe mongolism to be caused by triploidy of the twenty-first chromosome, we have no grounds for claiming that he fell victim to a racist mode of thinking. The inductivist explanation of scientific error is not only wrong but dangerous. It implies that men like White, Knox, and Down made mistakes because their hearts were not in the right place and that all we need today in order to avoid or combat racism is a pure heart. I believe that we also need a clear head.

There is also a functionalist explanation of scientific error, or at least of this particular kind of error. Harris writes: 'prior to the nineteenth century, nations had never rewarded their wise men to prove that the supremacy of one people over another was the inevitable outcome of the biological laws of the universe' (Harris 1968: 81). But, except perhaps for Nott, it is difficult to see that any of the originators of racist theories were rewarded for their handiwork. The truth, as Harris himself stresses, is that the beginnings of anthropology as a recognizable discipline are bound up with the theory of racial determinism and 'no major figure in the social sciences between 1860 and 1890 escaped the influence of evolutionary racism' (1968: 130). Scientific errors are being made all the time. It is what happens afterwards that matters. The scientific community is supposed to sort the grain from the chaff, but science as a form of social organization is heir to many weaknesses.

THE ATTRIBUTION OF RACISM

The definitions I reviewed at the beginning agree that racism is a pseudo-biological doctrine. The adjective 'racist' has however been applied in the past to persons and doctrines that made no direct reference to biology. Some racists, after all, have not been educated enough to manipulate such ideas; others have not worked out systematically the implications of their everyday thoughts. Nevertheless, it has often been safe to assume that if these people were pressed into systematizing their views they would be forced back on to pseudo-biological ideas. Whether we should continue to use the word racist in this way is now questionable.

Most previous writers have, in my view, insufficiently appreciated the extent to which racism originates in scientific error. I have tried to indicate how it was the product of a movement in biology that has been left far behind. As a biological doctrine, racism is dead. Consequential adjustments at the level of popular understanding can be observed in several countries. In the 1968 presidential campaign in the USA, ethnic group sentiments and loyalties could be evoked without mention of race. A speaker had only to refer to the need to maintain law and order and his listeners took this as a remark directed against Negroes. White Americans today do not need a doctrine to assuage guilt feelings over the treatment of the Negroes. Many of them feel threatened by Negro demands. White hostility functions so as to defend the privileged position which the whites have secured and believe they deserve. Whites seem on the whole to regard the issue as part of a power struggle; biological arguments excite little interest. In the United Kingdom, those who have argued most fiercely for the exclusion of coloured immigrants and were most critical of the legislation against discrimination have increasingly stressed the social difficulties hindering assimilation and have complained that in areas where the immigrants settle the character of the local community is destroyed. These critics have frequently been careful to disavow any belief in racial superiority and have not employed racist doctrine. In southern Africa, too, it seems as if policies implying the unequal treatment of ethnic groups are more and more defended on political and cultural rather than on pseudo-biological grounds.

Consider the following extracts from a recent book and see if you can guess the author:

'We are all of mixed race and the generalizations we use when we speak of races are merely for convenience. The Negro is not of one race but a mixture of races. So is the Caucasian and the Mongoloid . . . Blood transfusions of the correct blood groups can be given to members of any race . . . Groups such as the Aborigines of Australia who had been cut off from other races for centuries were able to interbreed with the White settlers. The facts prove conclusively that any doctrine of racial superiority is completely unfounded . . . any doctrine which preaches the superiority of one race over another is specious, evil nonsense . . .'

The author is Peter Griffiths, MP for Smethwick from 1964 to 1966 (Griffiths 1966: 15, 61).[2]

Many factors may contribute to group hostility. It is a commonplace that emotional identification with one group often entails hostility towards others and that people will seek a rationalization for sentiments of this kind. It may be that when men have appealed to ideas of racial superiority, their arguments were not the outcome of beliefs about biology. If so, it would be foolish of us to waste our powder attacking a rationalization. If today those who seek to defend ethnic inequality are in search of an intellectual justification, will they turn, like their predecessors, to biology? I doubt it. There are many signs that they are turning to psychology, sociology, and social anthropology. Sociologists have shown, especially by their work in the educational field, that inequality can be transmitted from generation to generation by social mechanisms. So an educated man who wishes to exclude minority members from the privileges of the majority may turn for justification to the evidence accumulated by educational psychologists. In a new American book on segregationist thought, the editor states:

'Only extremists, who embarrass other segregationists, still insist that Negroes are absolutely inferior to Whites, or openly justify violence and intimidation to keep the race subordinate. The emphasis now is on racial differences. Races are said to differ in relative abilities in different areas of endeavour. Thus Whites might be superior in some areas – intelligence, reasoning, and adaptability to Western civilization, for example – and Negroes in others – rhythm, perspiration and domestic art.'

He cites a legal action against school integration in Georgia in which the white applicants argued, 'Existing ethnic group differences in educational achievement and psychometric intelligence are of such a magnitude that extensive racial integration will seriously impair the academic standards and educational opportunities for the petitioners and other White children of Savannah-Chatham County' (Newby 1968: 10).

Another area of research to which appeal may be made in the future is that of ethology. Mr Enoch Powell, in his speech of 9 June 1969, referred to an instinct to preserve an identity and defend a territory as 'one of the deepest and strongest implanted in mankind'. He added, 'I happen to believe that the instinct is good and that its beneficent effects are not exhausted.' To explain in this way the antipathy some Britons feel towards immigrants is also to justify it. Otherwise Mr Powell has made little or no use of biological arguments. It is more characteristic that in his Eastbourne speech of 16 November 1968 he apparently drew upon an article in the September 1968 issue of *Man* (the organ of the Royal Anthropological Institute) to stress the extent to which immigrant communities in Britain are still oriented towards the countries of origin. If the battle is shifting to another front, this does not mean that we can neglect the possibility that people may take biological findings concerning inheritance out of their context and use them for political ends. The only safeguard is a better understanding, throughout the population, of biological principles. This is needed as a safeguard against doctrines of class superiority as well as of racial superiority. We need better biology teaching for its own sake. We need better sociology teaching for its own sake. To choose little bits of either biology or sociology and publicize them in isolation is inadequate as a long-term programme for combating misrepresentation.

If indeed it is the case that those who would deny equal treatment to members of ethnic minorities now appeal primarily to cultural instead of biological variation, should we describe their views as racist? We may get an emotional satisfaction from doing so but there is a danger that such usage may conceal the changing nature of the tendency we wish to combat. By using it too readily we run the risk of the boy who called 'wolf' too often (cf. Spearman 1968). Let us remember, too, that many social scientists have argued all along that it is unwise to use biological terminology when designating social categories. The categories of people whom we identify by racial labels share advantages or disadvantages because of the social significance vested in biological distinctions. On such grounds some argue that we should speak not of race relations, but of ethnic group relations. In any event, sociologists will all recognize that there are important similarities between the situation of racial minorities and of other minorities, religious, linguistic, and economic. There are many people in industrial societies who suffer from physical or social disablement and are trapped by their handicaps just as are members of racial minorities. The study of how they come to be trapped reveals important lessons about how the social and economic system works in some of its less public aspects. What minorities have in common may be more important than the distinguishing mark of race.

Some commentators have spoken of the 'changing nature of racism', but this is justified only if one defines it in terms of its function. I argue that if we label the new culturally based doctrines 'racist' we may mislead people. To call them 'racialist' is much preferable, but not an ideal solution. In my view these new arguments and sentiments are more accurately classified as forms of ethnocentrism. Does the label matter? There is a tendency to describe as racist arguments that coloured immigration should be even further reduced or that there will be unwelcome consequences

from earlier immigration. In a previous generation such conten-
tions might well have assumed pseudo-biological doctrines about
race. Today this is less likely. If we diagnose them as based on bad
biology our remedies will probably achieve little. I have argued
that such arguments are better seen as part of a wider tendency to
appeal to new kinds of evidence and other sentiments so that they
are more accurately designated by a non-biological adjective. But
this is not to imply that new-style ethnocentrism is any better than
old-style racism. We must not tie our concepts to the expression of
approval or disapproval.

The study of race and race relations has been influenced at every
turn by political considerations and the personal values of research
workers. At one time scientific research on racial differences was
widely exploited for political ends. Today the pressure is much
the same but on balance the political ends have been reversed.
Racial hostility is identified as a threat to world peace. Social
scientists are called upon to try to eliminate it. Some, I think, have
been so keen to join the fray that they have misrepresented the
contribution that social science can make to the solution of political
problems. They have labelled some views and movements as
'racist', as if by so doing they were proving that they did not need
to be studied seriously. As Hughes says, this is exorcism. We
cannot exclude our values from our work, but we must be on our
guard for the ways in which they influence it. Not long ago the
principal philosophical position for the attack on intolerance
assumed that integration was the goal. Social scientists stressed
those bits of evidence which seemed to support an outlook of
benevolence, stigmatizing as 'baddies' those people who drew
attention to evidence that did not fit such an outlook. Now it
appears as if the integrationist flank has been turned by a new
programme which urges that equality can only be attained through
separation. We must remember that our moral outlooks are liable
to change and try to prevent our sociology from becoming dated
too quickly.

It has often been implied that sociology proves that equality is
better than inequality, but it is more truthful to admit that the
question of equality is an ethical and political matter. The social

sciences can, I believe, make a vitally important contribution to diagnosing the problem of inequality as it presents itself in different circumstances. They can illuminate the merits and demerits of different policies for dealing with inequality. But we must never allow others to shuffle on to the social sciences responsibility for political decisions. We must show that research can inform policy without suggesting that action against inequality should be delayed while we argue about racism and racialism. Nor should we imply that a government of sociologists could eradicate racial prejudice and discrimination.

Notes

1 The address as given to the conference was printed, with a few alterations, in *New Society*, no. 341, 10 April 1969, pp. 551–4. For purposes of publication in this volume it has been revised in certain respects while retaining the form of an oral address.

2 It was he whom the then Prime Minister accused of conducting a squalid campaign based on racial appeals, prophesying that he would 'until a further General Election returns him to oblivion, serve his term here as a Parliamentary leper'.

References

AGASSI, JOSEPH 1963. Towards an historiography of science. *History and Theory, Studies in the Philosophy of History*, Beiheft 2. 'S-Gravenhage: Mouton.

BANTON, MICHAEL 1967. *Race Relations*. London: Tavistock; New York: Basic Books.

BENEDICT, RUTH 1940. *Race and Racism*. London: Routledge.

COX, OLIVER CROMWELL 1948. *Caste, Class and Race: a study in social dynamics*. New York: Doubleday.

GLASS, BENTLEY, et al. (eds.) 1959. *Forerunners of Darwin 1745–1859*. Baltimore: Johns Hopkins Press.

GOSSETT, THOMAS F. 1963. *Race: the history of an idea in America*. Dallas: Southern Methodist University Press.

GOULD JULIUS., & KOLB, WILLIAM. L. 1964. *A Dictionary of the Social Sciences*. London: Tavistock Publications; New York: Macmillan.

GRIFFITHS, PETER 1966 *A Question of Colour*. London: Leslie Frewin.

34 *Michael Banton*

HARRIS, MARVIN 1968. *The Rise of Anthropological Theory*. London: Routledge.

HIRSCH, JERRY 1968. Behaviour-genetic Analysis and the Study of Man, pp. 37–48 in Margaret Mead, Theodosius Dobzhansky, Ethel Tobach, and Robert E. Light, eds. *Science and the Concept of Race*. New York: Columbia University Press.

HOCKING, GEORGE W., JR. 1968. *Race, Culture and Evolution: essay in the history of anthropology*. New York: Free Press.

HUGHES, EVERETT CHERRINGTON, & HUGHES, HELEN MCGILL 1952. *Where Peoples Meet: racial and ethnic frontiers*. Glencoe: The Free Press.

LÉVI-STRAUSS, CLAUDE 1952. *Race and History* (The Race Question and Modern Science series). Paris: UNESCO.

LIPSCHUTZ, ALEXANDER 1969. Review of Banton 1967. *Current Anthropology* **10** (2): 205–6.

MCPHEE, MALCOLM 1968. Review of Harris 1968. *Current Anthropology* **9** (5): 525.

NEWBY, I. A. (ed.) 1968. *The Development of Segregationist Thought*. Homewood, Ill.: Dorsey.

ROSE, PETER 1968. *The Subject is Race*. New York: Oxford University Press.

SIMPSON, GEORGE EATON, & YINGER, J. MILTON 1965. *Racial and Cultural Minorities*. 3rd edn. New York: Harper.

SNYDER, LOUIS L. 1962. *The Idea of Racialism: Its meaning and history*. New York: Van Nostrand (Anvil).

SPEARMAN, DIANA 1968. Enoch Powell's Postbag. *New Society*, 9 May: 667–9.

VAN DEN BERGHE, PIERRE L. 1967. *Race and Racism: a comparative perspective*. New York: Wiley.

JOHN REX

The Concept of Race
in Sociological Theory

THE POLITICAL IMPORTANCE OF A THEORETICAL
PROBLEM

The problem of race relations challenges the consciences of
sociologists in a way that probably no other problem does. Just
as physicists have been reminded of their social and political
responsibilities as the full meaning of nuclear warfare became
apparent, so sociologists, who are expected to understand the
relationships that exist between groups, have been confronted in
our own time with problems of racial conflict and racial persecu-
tion of a quite unprecedented kind. Before and during the Second
World War millions of Jews were exterminated, allegedly because
of their race, and with the support of a phoney kind of biological
and sociological theory. In our own day discrimination against,
or exploitation of, men distinguished by their skin colour prevents
millions of human beings from enjoying basic human rights. And
in the pattern of international history that is being woven for our
future, the one overriding theme seems to be that of race war.

In the world of 1945, still reeling from the experience of Nazism,
it was the biologists who were asked by the United Nations to
analyse the phenomenon of racism, and their work led to the
formulation of expert statements in 1941, 1951, and 1964. But,
while the biologists were able to answer the question, 'In what
sense does biological science distinguish races and other genetically based groups?' – a question that itself requires a highly
technical answer – they were not able to answer the separate
question, 'Why are groups of men between whom political differ-

ences exist sometimes called races?' All they could say was that such groups bore no relation to 'races' in the biological sense. The problem therefore was handed over to the sociologists (UNESCO 1969).

The problem with which we are faced is not, however, simply an empirical one. It is not a question, for example, of discovering what correlations there are between prejudice towards coloured persons, on the one hand, and a variety of other sociological indices, on the other. There have probably been more than enough studies of this kind already. The real problem is to distinguish among the various studies made by sociologists those which are distinguishable as race-relations studies. This is a complex *theoretical* question. It is one that must be answered, however, before any really systematic approach to the full range of situations leading to the growth of racism can be analysed. The fact that so little attention has been directed towards it can only be regarded as something of a professional scandal.

CURRENT DEFINITIONS OF THE FIELD OF RACE RELATIONS STUDIES

Before I proceed to make some preliminary suggestions as to how this field of study should be mapped, I should like to look at four separate approaches that seem to me, when taken individually, to be inadequate. When I have done this, however, I shall show that, taken together, they do help us to define the key variables of the race-relations field considered systematically.

The first of these approaches claims that there are no race-relations problems as such. All the problems with which race-relations experts deal, it argues, are really problems of stratification and, once these problems are fully understood, their racial aspect disappears.

There is a great deal to be said for this view, particularly if the term stratification is used in an inclusive rather than a narrow sense (referring not to classes in the Marxist sense or to hierarchically rated occupational groups but to all the kinds of differentiation and conflict that arise out of the military, political, and economic relations between men). It is certainly not sufficient to dismiss the whole group of theories involved here as 'Marxist'. But, none the less, there do seem to be aspects of what are called race-relations encounters which are not fully explained even by fairly flexible use of stratification theory, and the factor of role ascription and stereotyping according to observable characteristics does seem to add something new to these situations, as does their explanation and justification in terms of racist theory.

If, however, we turn to the second and third of the approaches made to the definition of their field by sociologists of race relations, we find that these too are inadequate if taken by themselves. If we say that race-relations problems arise when groups distinguish themselves in terms of perceived physical differences, we find that there are cases in which the perception of physical differences does not lead to race-relations problems and that, in any case, those who are classified as belonging to one group actually have a range for any characteristic that overlaps with the range for the same characteristic exhibited by another group (e.g. the darkest Sicilian might be darker than the lightest Negro). Moreover, such a definition excludes from the field the phenomenon of anti-Semitism, usually recognized as the outstanding expression of racism in our time.

Yet, if we simply try to confine our study as sociologists to the study of groups distinguished by cultural characteristics, nearly every phenomenon of culture contact comes within our field. The problem of the nationalisms that are to be found within and across national boundaries would certainly have to be included. So also would the study of religious minorities and the subculture of classes. Obviously, there must be some other feature of the situation in terms of which a subclass of racially defined situations can be distinguished.

Finally, we should note the existence of another approach that might loosely be called phenomenological. This approach recognizes that social phenomena and mental phenomena are meaningful and that the approach to discriminating any kind of structural situation must depend upon a consideration of 'definitions of the situation' used by participant actors. Hence it would seem that the problem disappears. If men typify a situation as racial, racial it must be, and all that the sociologist can do is to concentrate on the careful analysis of the structure of belief systems from which the concept derives. He cannot be expected to distinguish between false and true consciousness or between actually held and valid meanings.

The problem with this approach is not merely that it appears to sell the pass to the racists and to leave them to define the sociologist's field for him. It is that the complexity of meaning systems and their inextricable relations with structure are insufficiently explored. It is not surprising then that the real value of this approach only becomes evident when it is employed in conjunction with the other approaches mentioned above.

Similar problems arise in the use of the definitions suggested by Margaret Nicolson and referred to by Michael Banton.[1] According to Nicolson, 'racism is more often applied to the doctrine, racialism to the practice of the doctrine'. Such a terminology could either lead to a one-sided view of the cause of racialism, tracing it simply to false beliefs, or to a disjunction between the theory and the practice. The latter alternative is preferred by Banton, who suggests that we keep the term racism for the doctrine and that 'We can use racialism more widely to denote, for example, political policies which do not rely on biological ideas.'

If Banton's alternative is pursued, two consequences follow. In the first place no defining criterion of racialism, which distinguishes it from other political policies, remains. In the second place the definition of racism, since it refers only to theory, ceases to depend in any way on structural factors. Hence the only clearly demarcated field that remains is that of the study of ideas, and the problem of racism disappears as soon as politicians and others change their style of theorizing.

The approach taken here is as much against the study of theories in isolation as it is against the reduction of theoretical definitions of the situation to mere epiphenomena arising from structural sources. We envisage a two-way interplay between theoretical and structural factors. Or, putting this in another way, what we envisage is a combination of all four of the approaches mentioned above so that their genuine insights may not be outweighed by their one-sidedness. We therefore tentatively suggest the following definition:

> 'We shall speak of a race-relations structure or problem, in so far as the inequalities and differentiation inherent in a social structure are related to physical and cultural criteria of an ascriptive kind and are rationalized in terms of deterministic belief systems, of which the most usual in recent years has made reference to biological science.'

I believe that such a composite definition is the most useful one we could employ and that it has the merit of recognizing both the similarities and the differences between race-relations and other types of problem. What follows is a detailed explication and illustration of this definition.

Lest there should be any misunderstanding of our purpose here, it must be emphasized that we are by no means attempting to make an exact empirical report on the actual pattern of race relations in, say, the United States, Britain, or Latin America. In so far as we make reference to empirical and historical material in what follows we do so simply in order to clarify our typology by suggesting the questions to which it leads. We aim to draw up an agenda of possible studies, so that, with the questions better understood, we may be more aware of where the answers are likely to be found.

STRATIFICATION AND OTHER STRUCTURAL ASPECTS OF RACE-RELATIONS SITUATIONS

We said above that the notion that race-relations situations were explicable in terms of the theory of stratification had some validity, if the term stratification was used in an inclusive sense. I now wish to suggest that there are at least six kinds of situation that would have to be included. They are:

  1 Frontier situations, in which a politically organized group, with an advanced technology and education, encounters another such group whose levels of technology are lower.

2 The particular form of the social relations of production, which is to be found on slave plantations, and in the societies that come into existence immediately after the abolition of slavery.

3 Situations of class conflict in the Marxist, and in the rather wider Weberian, sense, where there is a confrontation of groups possessing differing degrees of market power.

4 Estate and caste systems, in which groups enjoying differing degrees of prestige and of legal rights take on a corporate character and may become occupationally specialized.

5 Situations in which esteem and prestige are not accorded to corporate groups, as such, but are thought of as providing a basis for a continuum, so that any one individual may be thought of as having more or less prestige.

6 Situations of cultural pluralism, such that a number of distinguishable groups interact for limited (e.g. economic) purposes but continue to lead separate communal lives.

Arising from these there appear to be a number of particular problems of metropolitan societies that are recurrently regarded as racial problems:

(*a*) Urban situations in which a complex system of 'stratification' based upon several of the factors mentioned above exists.

(*b*) Situations in which a particular group of outsiders is called upon to perform a role, which, although essential to the social and economic life of a society, is in conflict with its value system, or is thought to be beneath the dignity of the society's own members.

(*c*) Situations in which, in times of crisis, a group that is culturally or physically distinguishable is blamed for the existence of a threat to the society's wellbeing, i.e. scapegoat situations. This process is often connected with the structural situation under (*b*) above.

The first kind of situation listed is that which Toynbee refers to as characterized by the presence of an external proletariat. It existed when the 'barbarians' were at the gates of Rome, and it has existed on nearly every frontier during the expansion of

European nations overseas. It may lead to the extermination of the external proletariat, to their slow subordination and incorporation into the more advanced society, or to a more complex process in which the external proletariat is, militarily speaking, victorious but, culturally speaking, absorbed. Whatever the outcome, however, the encounter between the groups is marked by tension and by the emergence of stereotypes and belief systems that govern the interaction of members of one group with those of another. These may range from those based upon simple moral derogation, as in the case of Jan Van Riebeck's description of the Hottentots as 'dull, stupid, stinking people', through Aristotle's claim that the barbarian is less than a man, to modern theories that different moral characteristics derive from differing genetic inheritance.

Such frontier situations are one of the basic starting-points from which colonial societies emerge. Another alternative, however, is that in which the colonialist, as a part of his economic enterprise, introduces an alien labour force of varying degrees of freedom or unfreedom. Here the central institution is the slave plantation. Slave plantations are characterized by labour-intensive agricultural work and by the fact that the workers are owned by their employer. That is to say they are essentially productive enterprises. Racist belief systems are not necessary to their existence. Slave plantations existed in antiquity without being justified in racist terms, and it is clear that they have existed without masters and slaves being physically distinguishable. None the less, the capacity to regard other human beings as slaves does impose strains on the belief system of any society and bridging beliefs of some kind will nearly always be found. Racist beliefs are to be found in modern plantation situations as well as in the aftermath of abolition, and would seem to be meaningfully related to the legal and economic institution of slavery.

Turning from these colonial situations to what are more commonly thought of as problems of class and stratification, we find that the dominant theory, based upon experience of the race problem in the United States, was for a long time that of Lloyd Warner (1936), that the race-relations situation was best understood as caste in its incipient phase.

The distinguished Negro Marxist sociologist, Oliver Cromwell Cox (1959), has performed a useful service in reminding us, in opposition to this view, that a great many of the situations classified as racial in modern industrial societies are nothing more or less than class situations in the classic Marxist sense. Thus, for example, the black proletariat of South Africa is clearly distinguishable, both from the white owning class and from white organized labour, by the fact that it has a distinct relationship to the means of production. Equally, the almost permanently unemployed Negro youth of America's urban ghettos look more and more like a class in revolt.

One feature of this class-conflict aspect of race relations that is of the very first importance is the development of a militant or revolutionary Black Power movement on an international scale. The situation here appears to be analogous to that which Marx was suggesting when he wrote of the transition from a local trade-union consciousness to a world-wide revolutionary consciousness. In that case, as in this, we are not necessarily dealing with an actual organized revolutionary class, but the sort of quasi-group that arises from a belief in the existence of a common political destiny. In any case the study of this black-power revolution is central to the study of race relations.

Cox is perhaps wrong, however, in suggesting that class conflict has always been the determining factor in black–white relations. Underdeveloped societies and those undergoing one-sided development through agriculture and mining might well produce some of the main features of the social and political systems to which he attaches the terms caste and estate. The existence of legal inequality and inequality of esteem, together with the maintenance of the authority of a land-owning ruling class, has been a feature of some Latin American societies and it is this which leads some students to the view that a caste-like situation often underlies a problem that comes to be thought of as racial.

It is not sufficient to characterize such societies as paternalist (see, for example, Van den Berghe 1967). Indeed it is gravely misleading, for the actual relations between upper and lower 'classes' are often brutally exploitative. If they are distinguishable from what some sociologists call competitive situations, it is not because the lower orders regard their masters as fathers but because, as in medieval Europe, their social situation, and sometimes their _Paternal legal status, makes any challenge to the authority of their superiors impossible. It is this which leads us to the view that some race-relations situations are in fact based on caste and estate systems.

An objection might be made here by either Warner or Cox that in the case of true caste systems an exploitative element such as we have described is not present. We concede that this may be so in the Indian case. But no other society has attained a fully developed caste system, even by Warner's reckoning. The main point in our using the term is that estate systems mentioned above could develop in the direction of considerable occupational specialization. Where this occurs we may say that an estate system is developing in a caste-like direction.

Another feature of the Caribbean and Latin American situations, however, is the sheer fact of cultural pluralism brought about through the coming together of Negro, Asiatic, and European labour. It is not surprising, therefore, that the concept of the plural society first pioneered by J. S. Furnivall in Indonesia[2] has been applied there. According to Furnivall's ideal type, a situation might be expected in which ethnically distinct groups meet only in the market-place. And while relations there are based upon exploitation of the harshest sort, each group can and does withdraw to its own independent quarter, where it is not subject to the authority of the others.

In fact, most sociologists found that in applying this concept a measure of inequality of power and status extending beyond the market-place had to be accounted for, but this is not to say that the simple differentiated and pluralist society described by Furnivall is not useful, at least as an extreme ideal type against which degrees of inequality can be measured.

Again, while it is useful in order to grasp the flux and variety of historical experience, to see some Latin American and African situations as approximating to a feudal estate system, it is none the less clear that such a system nowhere exists in a pure form. What does seem to be the case, however, is that as a system of this kind or, for that matter, a plantation system becomes less and less perfect, it breaks down into a status system. Everyone is therefore allocated a certain standing in the society along a quantitatively varying status scale. Thus the position accorded to a man may be high or low according to the lightness or darkness of his skin.

Nearly all of the problems so far discussed are problems that have been encountered at one time or another by British people in their colonial dealings. What is new, however, is the fact of the emergence of a 'racial problem' in the cities of the metropolitan country itself. The more complex subcategories I have listed are intended to provide a framework for the analysis of this problem.

The first fact to notice about colonial immigrants in British society is that not only are they distinguishable on the basis of their skin colour, language, religion, and domestic culture but also they are known through these indicators to have come from fulfilling colonial roles to adopting the role of worker in the metropolitan society. Thus there is at the moment of encounter with the native metropolitan population a double-banked criterion for role ascription. With this said, however, it has still to be noted that relations between such a differentiated group and their hosts are further shaped by the nature and structure of the metropolitan society itself.

One feature of that metropolitan society that increasingly comes to notice, and has been even more clearly brought to notice by the arrival of immigrants, is the existence of a number of unwanted and low-status industrial roles. The more technological advance and educational levels make other kinds of work less arduous or more satisfying, the greater the relative deprivation of those who fulfil these roles. They are therefore shunned by native workers and an alien group can easily be assimilated into them.

Thus far in the British post-war experience, however, it has not been on the industrial front that the immigrant has faced the most acute conflict. Rather it has been with his neighbours in the city. Elsewhere it has been argued that the city can at least in part be analysed as a system of housing class conflict, modified by the emergence of a status-stratified neighbourhood system.[3] I suggest that it is within a system of this kind that immigrants already identified as colonials, and already marked by their past colonial roles, have to take up positions and to encounter their fellow citizens and workers. Of course, the problem comes to be defined as primarily a racial problem, but it should also be clear from what has been said that the pattern of interaction and conflict with which we are dealing here derives partly from the structure of colonialism and partly from the urban class system; neither of which is simply and solely a racial situation.

Taking together the two facts of the emergence of relatively deprived industrial roles and of deprived neighbourhoods, one can see that the immigrant worker is likely to be categorized as belonging to a pariah group, and, in times of crisis, made a scapegoat. Immigrants form pariah groups both in doing unwanted jobs and in providing a kind of housing and neighbourhood that the city needs but that its value system cannot allow it to tolerate. Along with other clearly visible minority groups (e.g. students), they can easily act as scapegoat to be blamed for any hardship suffered by majority groups.

Scapegoating is too often discussed as though it were a purely psychological phenomenon. True, the punishment of the scapegoat is a means of restoring mental equilibrium to those whose personality systems are disturbed. But scapegoating is also a means of restoring *social* equilibrium. Thus certain groups or individuals are threatened because of the hostility their actions or incompetence have engendered. The indication of a scapegoat is a social mechanism whereby resentment may be expressed and the existing power structure maintained. It is the social process *par excellence* that literally fulfils Parsons's description of one of his functional subsystems as pattern maintenance and tension management.

Pariah groups may exist without becoming scapegoat groups. Pariah status simply refers to the fact that the group's social function, though necessary, is held to be undesirable. The group may be hated and may even be punished. It does not, however, become a scapegoat unless or until it is blamed for acts it has not committed.

In most cases, of course, a pariah role does go with scapegoating. Jewish moneylenders in European history, the Asian trader in

Colonial Africa, the immigrant landlord in European cities, have all performed this double function. One part of it, the pariah part, lies in actually carrying out or even being forced to carry out certain duties and being punished for so doing. The other, or scapegoat part, consists in being held generally to blame for failures of the system.

THE ASCRIPTIVE BASIS OF ROLE ALLOCATION

What we have been trying to do thus far is to distinguish structures of social interaction of a major socio-political kind that may be associated with the notion of racial differentiation. In no case does the interaction take its character from the fact that men with perceptibly different physical characteristics (let alone of different biological races) are parties to the social encounter. What we are dealing with as a rule is the deployment of power by one group against another, whether that power be military, political, or economic. This is the point that those who argue that the study of race relations is simply a part of the more general study of stratification are seeking to emphasize.

Overemphasis on this point, however, might lead to the view that whether or not such structural situations become defined in terms of race is purely a matter of accident. This would be a mistake, for, while it is true that the rationalization and justification of power must depend in part on the belief systems available, and that some of these lend themselves more readily than others to providing justifications of a racist kind, it is also the case that *there are certain kinds* of 'stratification' situation that, belief systems apart, are more likely to develop into racially defined situations than others. That is to say, whether or not a 'stratification situation' leads to 'racial problems' depends in part on the particular nature of that situation itself and in part on ideological factors.

The functionalist view that all social structures must have some mechanism for the allocation of personnel to roles and that there is a broad divide between mechanisms based upon ascription and those based upon achievement seems to beg the question here. For it is rarely the case that we are simply dealing with an ongoing social system in which the choice between one mechanism and another is available. Mostly we are dealing with situations that have emerged out of colonial conquest and the absorption of one society by another or with situations of immigration by relatively powerless groups into established social systems. Hence the social systems involved have a hybrid character. The settlers and the natives in the one case, and the immigrants and their native-born hosts in the other, are easily distinguishable by physical or cultural characteristics, so that it is not surprising that in structures arising from their interaction sociologists claim that role allocation is ascriptive. It *is*, of course, ascriptive and this distinguishes these structures from others with 'open-class' systems. But the crux of the matter is the living together of groups with differing degrees of power in a plural society.

The important issues involved here are those raised by Franz Oppenheimer (1914) in his critique of the Marxian theory of the origin of the state. We need not go so far as to extend Oppenheimer's theory to argue that stratification is always and everywhere the result of conquest, but we can see that in many cases, directly or indirectly, a stratification system might be skewed from the pattern it might have been expected to follow had only 'internal' factors (i.e. relations to the domestic means of production) been involved. One of the indicators of such a situation is the existence of a situation in which role allocation appears to occur on an ascriptive basis.

It would be difficult to maintain a theory that some actual factor of conquest was always involved in ascriptive stratification situations, for the actual connection is sometimes tenuous, especially where we are dealing not with situations in colonial countries but with problems of immigration into the metropolitan societies themselves. None the less, we should insist that it is always the case that the groups who are parties to such a situation are differentiated in terms of their access to legitimate political power. This would apply as much to Jews in a country in which anti-Semitism flourishes as to immigrants from a colonial dependency.

We seem, in fact, to be concerned in race-relations studies with two broad classes of situation. One is that which arises directly from the business of colonial conquest and which involves the assignment of the conquered to the most menial roles. The other is the case in which, either in a metropolitan or in a colonial society, an alien group of immigrants, culturally or physically distinguishable from the rest of the population, are allowed or required to perform what in the society's own terms are morally questionable roles. The unifying social theme is that groups of differing ethnic or national origins live together in a single socio-economic system in circumstances where some of the groups involved have less access than others to legitimate political power.

THE NATURE AND ROLE OF RACIST BELIEF SYSTEMS

The presence of these two factors (i.e. in the broadest sense of the term, a 'stratification' factor and the possibility of ready classification of those who perform different social roles in terms of some simple ascriptive criterion) is, according to the view adopted here, a necessary condition for the emergence of a race-relations problem. That is to say, we are arguing that any attempt to explain the structure and dynamics of race-relations situations in terms of the strangeness of the newcomer, of culture shock, or in terms of immigrant and host, is inadequate if taken by itself. We would insist that without the power or stratification element there would be no race-relations problem.

On the other hand, it must be pointed out that neither 'stratification' taken by itself, nor even stratification coupled with role allocation in terms of ascriptive criteria, is by itself sufficient reason for describing a problem as a race-relations problem. The other necessary condition is that the belief systems in terms of which roles are explained, described, and justified should have a particular character. In other words, it is not possible to give an adequate and complete account of a race-relations situation without reference to the fact of racism. Even if it could not be argued that racist beliefs played an independent causal role within the total structure, it would still be the case that a complete description and analysis of that structure required a consideration of racism and its relation to structural factors. As we see it, however, racism has a double importance as a part of the total situation and as having an independent causal role in the dynamics of stratification and race-relations structures.

All social situations depend for their character upon the definitions we give to them in our culture. We cannot see society or social institutions or social relations. We simply learn to accept that the occurrence of certain sorts of behaviour may be read as indicating the operation of a social institution or that the presence of a person with certain characteristics implies the existence of a certain pattern of rights. We do not, however, rest content with labelling the various sorts of social interaction in which we engage any more than we rest content with a world of discreet physical things. We grope after anchoring and validating principles that explain why things are as they are and why they should be so. Myth and theology, philosophy and science, all provide us with systematic ways of meeting this need.

There are, however, two quite distinct kinds of belief system that, for lack of a better word, we may call deterministic and undeterministic. When the former are applied to the justification of a social structure the social structure comes to be seen as inevitable and unalterable, and transition from one kind of role to another may be held to be impossible.

The clearest example of such a deterministic theory is the one to which the term racist is most often confined. What happens in this case is that the fact that a particular group suffers discrimination is attributed to an incapacity to perform a role or a special capacity to behave in particular ways that is determined by genetic inheritance. This is the most completely deterministic theory in that it is argued that nothing any individual can do can alter the situation and the pattern of rights in the society.

The specific problem of racism as it was posed to the United Nations in 1945 was concerned with a consideration of a belief system of this kind. It therefore seemed sufficient to gather together expert opinion to show that role performance in modern social systems did not depend upon man's genetic inheritance. This, however, left open a number of other possibilities and the disrepute into which racist theories in the narrow sense have fallen has simply meant that those who profited from them have sought other means of ideological support.

Long before justifications for inequality and exploitation were drawn from biological science they were drawn from theology. Indeed, it could be argued that it was only because the ideological extremism of nineteenth-century positivism demanded the justification of everything in terms of natural science, that biological theories assumed the predominance they did and that the decline of scientism would inevitably lead to the recurrence of other forms of theory. Theology, it is true, might play only a small part but *sociological* doctrines about the superiority of particular cultures and social systems might come to play their part. Thus we should not take the disappearance of the specifically biologically oriented theories of race that were so important in the thirties to mean that the class of sociological problems to which they referred has disappeared. Other deterministic theories would still be used and the essential distinguishing feature of this class of situations, namely inequality between men being justified in a deterministic way, would still be present.

Thus we seem to have arrived at a clearer understanding of the specific field of study with which the sociology of race relations should be concerned. It is concerned with a broad range of stratification situations (using this term in a wide sense to include any situation in which power and privilege are unequally distributed between groups or individual role-players in a social structure), but only in so far as roles or group-memberships are ascribed in terms of observable physical or cultural characteristics such as those which distinguish groups of colonial conquerors and conquered and only if the system as a whole is justified by deterministic beliefs.

It should perhaps be pointed out here that the distinction between deterministic and undeterministic belief systems is not absolute and that deterministic assumptions might well be found hidden in a theory of an undeterministic kind. Thus it may be said that a group of people are not yet ready in terms of education or economic advancement to assume equal rights, but if it is also held that the group concerned cannot be expected to advance economically or educationally during 25, 50, or 100 years, the belief operates deterministically Furthermore, it might well be that, while the implicit belief of a governing group might be that the governed are inferior from a biological or theological point of view, their explicit statements might all refer to non-ascriptive criteria of role allocation. In this case the sociologists' task would not merely lie in describing the structure and the explicit belief system in terms of which it was justified (a process that itself has the character of unmasking or demystification); it would first involve the discovery or unmasking of the implicit theory that itself had to be unmasked by reference to the actual social structure.

THE INDEPENDENT CAUSAL ROLE OF BELIEF SYSTEMS

A further group of problems is suggested, however, by the definition at which we have now arrived. This may be described in the language of Marxism as assessing the relative causal role in race-relations situations of basis and superstructure, or of the stratificational and power element on the one hand and the ideological element on the other. We suggest that, although the existence of some kind of stratificational problem is a necessary precondition of the emergence of a race-relations problem, it is not by itself a sufficient condition. A further precondition is the existence of certain kinds of belief system. Moreover, it must further be recognized that once a deterministic belief system is used to justify a particular stratification situation, that situation is itself changed thereby and the belief system may set in motion wholly new social processes.

Of some importance with regard to the development of stratification situations in a racist direction is the sort of religious or political ideology that is available. Thus it does seem to be the case that race looms less large as a problem in Catholic countries because Catholic social teaching is inhospitable to the notion of deterministic differences between men, and in this may be contrasted with Calvinism, which contains within itself the deterministic distinction between the elect and the damned. Equally, it could be that Marxism as a political philosophy may not be made

c

readily compatible with racialism. A great many comparative and case studies would have to be made, however, before a conclusion on this problem could be reached, and it would be of particular importance to look at deviant cases, i.e. those in which, say, Catholicism or Marxism was redefined in practice to allow for racial discrimination.

But ideological factors may not serve merely to arrest or facilitate the development of racial discrimination. They may, in Marxist terms, 'take on a life of their own'. As we have already seen, they may lead to the social process of punishing a scapegoat group and this will in turn lead, as Myrdal has pointed out, to increased hostility and discrimination and hence to increased demands for punishment.

Even this hypothesis, however, is compatible with an ebb or flow in the intensity of scapegoating according to the intensity of a social, political, or economic threat. What is often overlooked, however, is that although the tide of racism continues to flow after it has started and may flow more or less slowly according to the structural situation, it may not ebb at all, unless action is taken on the ideological level. Thus to point the issue in terms of Britain's predicament in 1969, the racism that has been evident in the community since the speeches of Mr Enoch Powell and others might have arisen from the failure of the social and economic programmes of successive governments and the need for a scapegoat, but, once started, racism has threatened to become a regular election issue and a regular political theme.

If it is recognized that the ideological factor does make a difference in its own right, however, there is cause for optimism as well as pessimism among liberals on race-relations matters. True, what we have called Powellism may outrun even the functional need of the social system for a scapegoating mechanism. But equally it is possible that alternative beliefs authoritatively stated by political leaders will have a braking effect. This is not, of course, a purely ideological battle and the core of an anti-racist programme must lie on the structural level. None the less, words, speeches, and political actions also matter, either for the intensification or for the abatement of racial discrimination, exploitation, and conflict.

What we are saying in effect is that, even after we have given a comprehensive structural account (including under the heading 'structural' not merely patterns of social relations, but also the belief systems and ideologies that are intimately interwoven with them) of possible race-relations situations, we should still have to study racism, both in the way in which it varies in relation to changes in the structural base and as an independent factor with a possible cumulative effect on social structures. Indeed, in circumstances like that in contemporary Britain, it might be that this type of study should have priority over all others.

CONCLUSION: THE CENTRAL ROLE OF THEORY AND
COMPARATIVE STUDIES IN RACE-RELATIONS RESEARCH

The programme and definition of the field that we have suggested for race-relations research is in no way remarkable. Indeed, it would appear to conform to the sociological procedure outlined by Durkheim when he suggests that in the study of any social phenomenon we should,

'indicate first of all by what characteristic one might recognize the thing so designated, then classify its varieties, investigate by methodical inductions what the causes of its variation are, and, finally, compare these results in order to abstract a general formula' (Durkheim 1950: 25).

The really surprising thing is that so little of the sociology of race relations in Britain has conformed to this plan of attack.

The principal obstacle to the development of this programme has probably been quite simply and quite discreditably a disinclination on the part of some sociologists to look at race-relations problems in ways that might be disturbing to the liberal political establishment. Clearly, though, if the assumptions outlined here are correct, the study of race relations is, among other things a part of political sociology. This must mean that when we consider race-relations problems in Britain, the behaviour of governments and the policies advocated by all political parties must be up for description and analysis along with other phenomena. We cannot

simply assume that there is a basic situation of good will in Westminster or Whitehall and that what we have to do is merely to
test particular hypotheses as part of a programme of piecemeal
social engineering. All too often this is precisely what sociologists
have been asked or encouraged or have undertaken to do.

This response has necessarily led to trivialization of sociological
concepts in the race-relations field. But sometimes trivialization
seems to have been chosen for its own sake. Thus, although I
believe that there is a great deal of scope within an overall framework such as I have outlined for micro-sociological studies, too
often the cart has been put before the horse and potentially useful
concepts referring to immigrant–host relations, to the stranger and
colour–class hypotheses, to role theory and to status-crystalliza-
tion, have been used as though they by themselves provide a
sufficient theoretical foundation for the study of race relations. I
find it difficult, myself, to regard work such as this as professionally
serious.

I believe that in the field of race relations what we are faced with
today is a test of our professional integrity, of our capacity to
pursue an objective and systematic programme of sociological
study. The area of race-relations research is and will continue to be
politically sensitive and those who work in it will be under con-
tinual pressure to confine themselves to undertaking only those
studies or producing only those conclusions which are least disturbing to government. Work of an alternative kind has only
just begun. The object of this paper is to urge that we agree on our
theoretical programme and then set out to produce the research
workers and to create the necessary institutions to carry it out.

Notes

1 See Michael Banton's paper on 'Racism' in *New Society*, April 1969.
2 J. S. Furnivall (1948). For a further discussion of the concept of the
  plural society, see M. G. Smith (1965).
3 J. Rex and R. Moore (1967). For detailed statistical evidence on the
  distribution of coloured immigrants in Britain, see C. Peach (1968).

References

BANTON, MICHAEL 1969. What do we mean by Racism. *New Society*, 9 April.

COX, OLIVER CROMWELL 1959. *Caste, Class, and Race*. New York: Monthly Review Press.

DURKHEIM, E. 1950. *Rules of Sociological Method*. Glencoe, Ill.: The Free Press.

FURNIVALL, J. S. 1948. *Colonial Policy and Practice*. London: Cambridge University Press.

OPPENHEIMER, F. 1914. *The State*. Indianapolis.

PEACH, C. 1968. *West Indian Migration to Britain*. London: Oxford University Press.

REX, J., & MOORE, R. 1967. *Race, Community, and Conflict*. London: Oxford University Press.

SMITH, M. G. 1965. *The Plural Society in the British West Indies*. Berkeley: University of California Press.

UNESCO 1969. *Four Statements on the Race Question*. Paris.

VAN DEN BERGHE, P. L. 1967. *Race and Racism*. New York: Wiley.

WARNER, W. LLOYD 1936. American Class and Caste. *American Journal of Sociology* 42: 234–7, Sept.

DAVID LOCKWOOD

Race, Conflict, and Plural Society[1]

Despite the dominating importance of the racial problem in both
national and international affairs, the concept of race has not
played a central role in the development of modern social theory.
The fact that the study of race relations has been relatively isolated
from the mainstream of sociological analysis is regarded as a grave
disadvantage for the subject by some scholars, who attribute this
shortcoming to a lack of concern with race on the part of the
founders of the sociological tradition.[2] Yet, given the nature of
this tradition, it was inevitable that race could not emerge as a
key concept of sociological explanation.

To begin with, it may be noted that no racial problem at all
comparable to that of the present day presented itself in the historical situation in which the basic structure of sociological theory
took shape. But this is of perhaps less significance than the fact
that the attempts to provide explanations of social phenomena in
terms of racial properties that were advanced during this same
formative period of modern sociology did not, except in a negative
way, make any contribution to the founding of a distinctive sociological discipline. For the development of the latter precluded,
from the outset, biological and other forms of non-social 'reduc-
tionism' and led instead to attention being concentrated on such
basic and universal aspects of social systems as religion and the
division of labour, whose interrelations provided the subject-
matter of theories that aimed at explaining social facts in terms of
other social facts. Thus, quite apart from not being confronted by
any racial problem as a national political issue, the creators of
modern social theory were committed from the start to a mode of
analysis in which a concept such as race could be of only secondary
importance.

Once the study of sociology came to be focused, at any rate at a theoretical level, on the universal, constitutive properties of societies in general, the essential social facts could legitimately be abstracted from the accidental. This strategy is clearly stated, for example, in the introduction to Durkheim's account of the 'elementary' forms of the religious life. In a context more germane to the present discussion, it is also made explicit in the title of Schumpeter's essay on 'Social Classes in an Ethnically Homogeneous Environment', which epitomizes the tendency of most writers on social stratification to treat ethnic and racial divisions of a population as secondary, complicating factors in the analysis of social inequality, despite their substantive importance in particular societies.[3] There is a simple logic in this procedure. Some lines of division are to be found in all societies but are of negligible importance as foci of group conflict (such as age and sex); whereas other lines of division may be of great importance in this respect but are not universally present (racial, ethnic, as well as some religious differences fall into this category). From this it is argued that by ignoring the necessary but unimportant, and the important but contingent, lines of division, the theorist is better placed to construct simple general propositions about the structure and functions of those inequalities of power and deference which are present in all societies, and in relation to which the 'complicating' features of ethnic, racial, or religious bases of stratification can be introduced at a later stage in the analysis. From this point of view, then – and its explicit or implicit acceptance by most writers on social stratification is very striking – the category of race is excluded from the formulation of general theories of social inequality.

Further, given the basic maxim that social facts are to be explained in terms of other social facts before recourse is had to non-social reductionist explanations, the introduction of the concept of race – even as a secondary, 'complicating' factor – has meant that race has been treated not as a phenomenon *sui generis* but rather as a special case of more general sociological concepts. This in turn means that socially significant differences in the conduct, motivation, and capacity of racial groups are held not to be attributable to 'biological' factors, and also, and more importantly, that the physical visibility[4] of the groups in question is not, in principle, a major obstacle to the establishment of racially irrelevant forms of interaction. That is to say, racial discrimination is seen essentially as the outcome of an historical cumulation of social and economic and cultural disadvantages that have made the racial minority at once visible as a 'status-disqualified' group and as a section of the community most vulnerable to class exploitation. Thus to the questions posed by Blalock (1967: 201):

> 'To what degree are race and class attitudes essentially interchangeable? Can both types of attitudes be analysed in terms of the same theories, with race being simply one of a number of criteria used in designating class position, or are there important ingredients involved in one type of attitude that do not appear in the other?'

the most general tendency would be to answer that race relations are to be analysed basically as class and status relations, even though the direct experience of the colour barrier constitutes a reality that defies and overshadows such an analytical dissection.[5] Empirically, however, it is difficult to give an unequivocal answer to the foregoing questions because even where some individuals from racially disprivileged groups have achieved substantial social and economic advances – as in Brazil – the overall relationship between stratification and colour persists, and the position of the upwardly mobile minority is, so to speak, contaminated by this general distribution.[6] Only if there were an approximation to a situation in which different racial and ethnic groups were distributed equally within the socio-economic hierarchy could any effect on social interaction of racial visibility *per se* be dissociated from the effects of other criteria of rank. To say that colour only symbolizes the fact that in most cases the characteristic feature of a racial minority is its immobilization in a 'lower-class' position on all dimensions of social rank is, therefore, premature; and it may underestimate the implications for social relations of those inveterate moral, aesthetic, and sexual connotations of colour which, as Fanon has shown, are part and parcel of the very terms of everyday language.[7]

However, the view that racial differences, considered purely as socially relevant physical characteristics, are of secondary importance to marked inequalities of class and status, is shared by writers of widely divergent theoretical persuasion.[8] Thus, for example, Parsons is in agreement with Baran and Sweezy in defining the problem of the Negro American as one of a 'lower-class status' and in perceiving the solution of this problem as being inextricably bound up with the fate of the whole of the lower class of American society. Parsons, of course, sees the solution in essentially Durkheimian terms: the Negro can be brought into full membership of the societal community through a planned process of 'inclusion' analogous to that which has been achieved more or less spontaneously by other immigrant groups. The key mechanism of such a process of inclusion is the implementation of the 'social' rights of citizenship, which, together with civil and political rights, may be regarded as the substantive conditions of what Durkheim meant by 'organic solidarity'. By making possible their *de facto* rather than simply formal legal opportunity of participation in the larger community, American Negroes will become included within the existing socio-economic system without losing that sense of group identity and cultural distinctiveness which is part of the American pluralistic tradition. Such a change, however, is only part of a wider civic incorporation which is necessary in order to bring 'not only the Negro but the whole of the lower class into the societal community'. In the present situation

> 'The Negro, in becoming only a "special case", even if a very salient one, loses a ground for special consideration which he has enjoyed. At the same time, he has established a position for tapping much wider bases of support than before. He can become the spokesman for the much broader category of the disadvantaged, those excluded on this egregious ground. The Negro movement, then, can become the American style "socialist" movement.'

Considering the massive redistribution of economic resources that would be entailed (though Parsons characteristically accords to the economic system a relatively low degree of inertia in his value-controlled model of 'cybernetic change') by such a change, this view of the 'inclusion' process may appear rather optimistic. However, the main point to be stressed here is the way in which Parsons relates racial discrimination to a particularly acute class problem from which American society can no longer be protected by the 'fact of the immigrant status of the lower class' and by the process of upward mobility of lower-class immigrant groups that hitherto 'alleviated potential class problems'. In this respect, Parsons's position is not basically different from Marxist interpretations of the Negro problem. But of course, in the latter case, the solution of the racial class situation is not regarded as one that is possible within the framework of the existing socio-economic order. Nevertheless, it too involves a class- rather than a race-based movement.

> 'The black man alone should not bear the burden of restructuring America, and the immediate orientation of Black Power is toward altering the master–slave colonial relationship that is found in the ghetto. As such, it represents a temporary separatist stage directed against the immediate exploitation of the black community and to prepare the black masses, organisationally and psychologically, to enter into coalition with those other sectors of America which are ready to move towards radical change for all America . . . in America one is confronted with an oppressed racial minority which must ally itself with other groups if it is to stand any chance of restructuring the system by revolution' (Adler 1968: 96).

It is not the task of the present paper to enter into discussion of the relative merits of the two rival arguments. It is sufficient to stress the important area of theoretical consensus between them, and to emphasize the degree to which in the two most influential types of contemporary macro-social theory the category of race becomes to all intents and purposes, as Van den Berghe puts it, 'an epiphenomenon devoid of intrinsic significance' (Van den Berghe 1967: 94).

If the situation of a racial group *as a whole* can be analysed in terms of general sociological categories, the latter can also be used to explain variations in attitudes and behaviour *within* racial groupings. Thus while a low position on all main dimensions of social rank may characterize the general situation of a racial minority, there are subgroups of the minority whose location is best understood not in terms of the superimposition of disadvantage and derogation but rather by status inconsistency or incongruency. It has been shown that Negroes who rank high on occupational and educational criteria are more likely to be militant (at any rate in the Civil Rights movement) than those who are low-ranking in these respects or those who are high on one dimension and low on the other (Marx 1968: 57 et seq.). Again, among the white majority, those persons who are consistently high on various criteria of rank have more favourable attitudes to Negroes and are more ready for desegregation than are those persons who are rank-inconsistent (Tumin 1958: 195–6). Such examples of the application of familiar sociological principles could be multiplied; but to do so is unnecessary in order to establish the central point: namely, that no special concepts and generalizations have been required to account for observable differences in the behaviour of racial subgroups.

*   *   *

Against the thesis that no special sociological categories are necessary to explain the structure and dynamics of race relations, one very important critique has emerged: that which centres on the concept of 'plural society'. First developed in relation to ethnically and racially mixed societies, this concept has been given a more general scope by writers such as Berreman (1967), Braithwaite (1959–60), and Van den Berghe (1967) so as to include societies with pronounced caste and class divisions. More significantly, the idea of a plural society has been worked out in explicit opposition to theories that postulate consensus on common values as a prerequisite of social integration. Therefore the concept of plural society merits special attention if only because it might be regarded as an example of the introduction of concepts into general sociology that have emerged from the study of race relations, and thus as a refutation of the argument advanced in the first part of this paper.

Most generally, a plural society is conceived of as being 'compartmentalized into quasi-independent subsystems' on the basis of cultural and/or social segmentation (Van den Berghe 1965: 268–70) Cultural pluralism 'results from the presence within a given society of several ethnic groups, or, at least in the minimum case, of several distinguishable varieties of the same cultural tradition (such as class-based subcultures)', whereas social pluralism 'exists to the extent that a society is structurally compartmentalized into analogous and duplicatory but culturally-alike sets of institutions, and into corporate groups which are differentiated on a basis other than culture' (Van den Berghe 1967: 35). In the most extreme case the subsystems of a plural society have only highly specific points of contact with each other, such as common participation in a money economy and subjection to a common body politic. In this sense a plural society is distinguished from both a society integrated around a system of commonly shared values and a society integrated 'pluralistically' through the intersection of multiple lines of cleavage.

The claim of some proponents of the concept of plural society that this idea represents a radical innovation in dominant sociological theory is only true with respect to that body of thought which attributes overriding importance to the function of common values for social integration. The latter emphasis derives of course from the work of Durkheim, who, in virtually identifying society with a church, found it impossible to think of the coexistence of two rival moral communities within the same society. For this reason, in his theory of anomie it was the process of social declassification resulting from the breakdown of a single collective morality, rather than an ideological conflict between opposing classes, which represented the extreme case of social disorder. However, within the Marxist tradition of social theory, it is exactly the latter possibility (at least in analytical terms) of class-based ideological dissension that has provided a conception of social conflict diametrically opposed to that of Durkheim and his followers. Indeed, the work of Lenin and Gramsci in particular may be regarded as a formulation of the ideological and organizational conditions under which a society might approximate the revolutionary disorder of 'a church within the church'.

From this point of view, the concept of plural society is less of a novel contribution to social theory, and, in several respects, it poses less fundamental issues of sociological analysis. This is mainly because the cultural pluralism of ethnically, racially, or linguistically divided societies originates exogenously through the physical movement into the indigenous society of one or more culturally distinct groups, whose presence then results in the juxtaposition of separate blocs. On the other hand, the Marxist idea of a revolutionary society refers to a process of internal change whereby economic, or 'profane', conflicts arising from the structure of differentially related life-chances and life-experiences within a given division of labour come to be articulated into an ideological, or 'sacred', conflict about the legitimacy of the structure itself. Thus classes are located within a common division of labour and the ideological conflict between them takes shape within a common system of values and beliefs. In both these respects the bifurcation of society through class revolution may be distinguished from that which obtains in the case of conflict between racial or ethnic blocs in a plural society.[9] In the latter, conflict will tend to centre on the dominance of one group over another rather than on the system of domination as such. So that by contrast with class revolution, conflict in plural society, however violent, is not first and foremost directed at an alteration in the structure of power and deference but rather at the usurpation of power and deference by one section of the community to the disadvantage of the other. Ethnic and racial conflict has this orientation primarily because it is in the nature of the experience of the relationships of the majority and minority groups that the salient 'cause' of disaffection inheres in the given and unalterable properties of individual actors and not in the contingent properties of social systems. Because of this, racial and ethnic conflict is more akin to rebellion in ethnically and racially homogeneous societies in which the social order is likewise regarded as ineluctable. Thus revolutionary goals are unlikely to emerge from the antagonisms of groups in plural societies unless ethnic and racial divisions happen to coincide with lines of economic and other power relationships. Yet even when this coincidence obtains, it by no means always follows that the equation of race or ethnicity with class position leads to forms of conflict in which the latter element predominates over the former. And where this coincidence is lacking, the racial or ethnic identification usually overrides the consciousness of a common class position.[10]

There are, nevertheless, certain respects in which minority groups in both plural and class societies are frequently constrained to develop along similar lines: and this is particularly true of the tendency to form segregated subcultures. For example, in the case of the pre-1914 German Social Democratic movement, working-class separatism became institutionalized to a high degree around a party-based associational life which was intended to carry a revolutionary ideology but which in fact operated very largely to duplicate and substitute for middle-class associations from which workers were excluded (Roth 1963: esp. Ch. IX). This kind of class subculture has many parallelisms with the surrogate institutions of the 'black bourgeoisie' in the United States and with the ghetto-based 'nationalism' of the Black Muslims (Frazier 1962; Essien-Udom 1966: esp. Ch. 4). In practice if not in theory, and for their mass membership if not their leadership, such associations provide a means by which groups who in some way are lacking in social honour can protect themselves against this status depreciation and seek an alternative source of social worth. The institutionalization of class, ethnic, and racial subcultures or contra-cultures, with varying degrees of deviance from the dominant values of the society, is a common mode of adjustment of disadvantaged groups that are subject to a system of domination whose structure is unshakeable or for which no alternative is conceivable.[11]

While other similarities between the positions of subordinate class and racial groupings could no doubt be identified, the distinction between class conflict and the ethnic or racial conflict of a plural society remains a basic one. And it is from this perspective that the designation of the Black Power movement in the United States as a revolutionary movement is of particular interest. Black–white relations in that country have been characterized as a case of markedly developed social pluralism but of only minimal cultural pluralism (Van den Berghe 1967: 66). The decisive question, then, would appear to be whether, given its social segregation, the Negro community can be mobilized around an ideology which would be revolutionary by comparison with both the ghetto subculture of despair and the civil rights 'integrationist' policies of its middle-class leadership.

The conditions that have brought such a question to the fore are well known: and among them are not only the growing disillusionment of the Negro created by the slowness of integration relative to his aspirations but also the tendency to reject the goal of unilateral integration itself as incompatible with a new consciousness of racial dignity. The continuing concentration of the black population in the ghetto as an 'internal colony' of the dominant white society simultaneously provides what has been regarded as a natural base for the Black Power movement. At the same time, critics of this concept have stressed the extent to which the goal of civil rights still predominates within the black community and the degree to which Negro interests have become tied into the complex patterns of grass-roots politics in ways that could form a powerful obstacle to a national racial unity.[12] While such considerations are of obvious significance, they perhaps understate the possibilities of collective action that can be produced by the eruption of strong racial sentiments capable of transcending intra-group differences of occupation and diversity of local attachments. In the present situation it may be that the politics of millenarianism provide a more appropriate model for analysing the pattern of Negro protest than the conventional politics of pluralism.

From the present point of view, however, the question of whether the Black Power movement has a viable social base is less important than that of whether, given the lack of coincidence between racial and class divisions, it is possible for the potential mass membership of the Black Power movement to become activated by a revolutionary ideology. For the most extreme formulation of black-power doctrine draws on the analogy between the ghetto and the colony and leads to the conclusion that the goal of the movement is to de-colonize the ghetto and establish a vanguard of black socialism in the heartland of white capitalist America.[13]

The ideology of revolutionary black power thus not only defines the Negro as revolutionary but the revolution – at least initially – as Negro. The latter concept implies that whatever alliances might be made with radical forces in the white population must be made on equal terms, from a position of established black power. Indeed, it is only through the success of a separate, autonomous black movement that even white radicals can be brought into a full consciousness of the extent to which their own situation is privileged by the existing system of institutional racism. This strategy naturally stands in a relationship of some tension to Marxist theory, which, while accepting that racial revolution might preclude class revolution, nevertheless insists on the abandonment of purely racial interests and their translation into supra-racial, class interests as the only possible, long-run basis of a movement that is capable of introducing revolutionary change in a society where Negroes form a numerical minority and a relatively powerless economic bloc.[14]

In terms of sheer numbers, economic resources, and means of violence, the concept of the revolution as Negro is clearly untenable. But it is also necessary to question the further idea of the Negro as revolutionary, for this assumption of some black-power militants underlies the strategy of coalition with the white radical society that is frequently voiced. In particular, it may be asked whether the intensification of Negro protest would mean an increase in sentiments that favour the development of rebelliousness in a revolutionary direction. This question leads one back once again to the relative salience of class and racial consciousness in the conflicts that occur in a plural society, and in one where the working class is not coterminous with the black population. In this context, the emphasis given to the class element in the racial problem has perhaps been exaggerated by both white inclusionists and black revolutionaries. Just as the proponents of full integration for the Negro American may have underestimated the degree to which Negroes reject white society because of the humiliations attaching to colour as opposed to the deprivations of their lower class position, so too the advocates of black revolution may have overstressed the degree to which black militancy and solidarity reflects a revolt against class debasement as opposed to the stigma of race. Indeed, the more total and intense the conflict between black and white becomes, the more it is possible that that solidarity of the Negro population as a whole – and not just that of the lower class – will become focused on the symbol of colour. To the extent that this is so, the weaker will be the consciousness of class affiliations between racial groups and of class distinctions within the racial group. This means, in turn, that feelings of solidarity and antagonism are conditioned more by the immediate confrontation of actors who are defined for one another in terms of unalterable physical properties and less by the confrontation of ideas relating to the alterable properties of social systems. In short, it is conceivable that the more solid the black protest, the less of a potential for revolution this militancy provides. At any rate, this is the conclusion that the foregoing analysis points to, for if, as was suggested above, ethnic and racial conflict in plural society is not inherently revolutionary, then the idea of black power as black revolution involves a contradiction. If this is correct, then this contradiction, which arises from the application of an ideology of revolution to a movement whose cohesion is based to a large extent upon a sense of racial identity and community, should manifest itself in a considerable ambivalence in the appeals of the leadership. This would, indeed, seem to be the case. Both within the black-power leadership itself, and in its relations with white radicals, there is observable a marked alternation between the emphasis given to 'blackness' and 'unilateralism', on the one hand, and to 'socialism' and 'class unity', on the other.[15] To some extent, this must be attributed to sectarian struggles within both black and white camps; but it also reflects an obdurate social reality which the concepts of class and plural society may go some way in illuminating.

Notes

1 I wish to thank Elliott Isenberg and Sami Zubaida for their comments on this paper.
2 See, for example, Banton (1967: 62) and Van den Berghe (1967: 2–8).

It is noteworthy that 'race' does not appear in the indexes of either Nisbet's *The Sociological Tradition* or Coser and Rosenberg's reader in *Sociological Theory*, to take but two recent representative texts. In Parsons's *Structure of Social Action* there is one reference to race, and this briefly in relation to Durkheim's study of suicide.

3 Schumpeter (1951: 134): 'It is not meant to deny the significance of racial differences in explaining concrete class formations . . . but in order not to complicate the basic features of the picture, I thought it best to exclude the racial factor in what I have to say. When it comes to investigating the "essential" nature of a social phenomenon, it is often proper and necessary to ignore certain external factors that may be quite characteristic or at least common. They may be "essential" in many respects, but not for the purposes in hand.'

4 This is always in some degree socially determined, but not only in one direction. Compare the Brazilian saying that 'money bleaches' with Everett C. Hughes's observation that 'I do not go around looking for Negroes behind pale faces and blue eyes but I carry the experience of America in me' (Hughes 1965: 1138).

5 A comparison of, say, the excellent sociological study of the attitudes of American Negroes by Gary T. Marx (Marx 1968) and the work of Frantz Fanon (Fanon 1968) strikingly exemplifies this difference.

6 This 'general distribution' has of course an international as well as a national aspect (e.g. the effect on the position of the American Negro on the establishment of independent African states).

7 Again the Brazilian experience is instructive. Pierson's conclusion that 'prejudice exists in Brazil; but it is *class* rather than *racial* prejudice' has been qualified by Wagley who writes: 'In both the cities and the rural communities of north Brazil, there is a decided preference for Caucasian physical features', and 'the common Brazilian statement that "We Brazilians are becoming one people" seems to imply that Brazilians hope to become a nation more Caucasian in physical appearance. The process of absorption of the Negro into the white population discussed by Pierson, and the "bleaching" process mentioned by T. Lynn Smith, are both part of the unstated race policy of Brazil' (Wagley 1963: 153). On the historical origins of racial stereotypes, see Jordan (1968: especially Ch. 1).

8 The following quotations are from Parsons (1965). The other reference is to Paul A. Baran and Paul M. Sweezy (1966: Ch. 9).

9 A complete bifurcation of society into 'two great hostile camps' in this manner is, of course, an ideal case, which for several reasons is not an empirical possibility. But the same applies to the concept of a society in which there is universal commitment to a common value

system; and in so far as one analytical device is taken as a point of reference the other is logically implied as an opposite limiting case. It is also important to note that class revolution cannot be treated as a zero-sum power conflict. The aim of the revolutionary class is to reconstitute power relations in such a way as to alter the total production of power and not simply reallocate a given quantum of power in a different way. In this sense, the phenomenon of revolution involves a concept of power which, in general terms at least, is very close to that advanced by Talcott Parsons. For a useful summary and critique of the latter, see Anthony Giddens (1968).

10 See, for example, Leggett (1968: especially Chs. 6 and 7).

11 In an interesting extension of Weber's analysis of ethnic groups, Gertrud Neuwirth has argued that in the case of American Negroes it is their inability to acquire a sense of ethnic honour which has prevented them from achieving 'community closure', i.e. the monopolization of economic opportunities and political office, within the black community (Neuwirth 1969).

12 See, for example, James Q. Wilson (1965).

13 I fully realize that the concept of black power is shot through with ambiguity, which is in itself a social fact of prime importance. However, there is now a pronounced tendency among the most militant Negro groups to extend the concept so as to regard the goal of what Weber called 'community closure' as a *means* of reconstituting the black communities as socialist enclaves. See, for example, the comments of Stokeley Carmichael in his speech on 'Black Power' (Carmichael 1968: 161).

14 Adler (1968: 107) points out the inappropriateness of the analogy between ghetto and colony when he writes: 'In Third World revolutions, one finds oppressed racial and national minorities rebelling against a small colonial elite – all within the context of underdeveloped economies. However, in America one is confronted with an oppressed minority which must ally itself with other groups if it is to stand any chance of restructuring the system by revolution. If the first level, decolonisation, is pursued to the exclusion of the second, namely coalition, the black power movement will fail – that is unless one can foresee the possibility of a black U.S. Steel, General Motors, etc., which would provide the ghetto with a potent economic base to guarantee meaningful independence from White America.'

15 See, for example, Ronald Steel (1969), and the SDS Black Panther Party-Resolution, *New Left Review* (1969).

References

ADLER, FRANKLIN HUGH 1968. Black Power. *The Socialist Register.* London: Merlin Press.

BANTON, MICHAEL 1967. *Race Relations.* London: Tavistock Publications; New York: Basic Books.

BARAN, PAUL A., & SWEEZY, PAUL M. 1966. *Monopoly Capital.* New York: Monthly Review Press.

BERREMAN, GERALD. 1967. Stratification, Pluralism and Interaction: A Comparative Analysis of Caste. In *Caste and Race,* edited by A. de Reuck and Julie Knight. London: Churchill.

BLALOCK, HUBERT M. 1967. *Towards a Theory of Minority Group Relations.* New York: Wiley.

BRAITHWAITE, LLOYD 1959–60. Social Stratification and Cultural Pluralism. *Annals of the New York Academy of Sciences* (83).

CARMICHAEL, STOKELEY 1968. Black Power. In *The Dialectics of Liberation,* edited by D. Cooper. Harmondsworth: Penguin Books.

ESSIEN-UDOM, E. U. 1966. *Black Nationalism.* Harmondsworth: Penguin Books.

FANON, FRANTZ 1968. *Black Skin, White Masks.* London: MacGibbon & Kee.

FRAZIER, E. FRANKLIN 1962. *Black Bourgeoisie.* New York: Free Press.

GIDDENS, ANTHONY 1968. 'Power' in the Recent Writings of Talcott Parsons. *Sociology* 2 (3), Sept.

HUGHES, EVERETT C. 1965. Anomalies and Projections. *Daedalus,* Fall.

JORDAN, WINTHROP D. 1968. *White over Black.* Chapel Hill: University of North Carolina Press.

LEGGETT, JOHN C. 1968. *Class, Race and Labor.* New York: Oxford University Press.

MARX, GARY T. 1968. *Protest and Prejudice: A Study of Beliefs in the Black Community.* New York: Harper & Row.

NEUWIRTH, GERTRUD 1969. A Weberian Outline of a Theory of Community: Its application to the 'Dark Ghetto'. *British Journal of Sociology* 20 (2), June.

PARSONS, TALCOTT 1965. Full Citizenship for the Negro American. *Daedalus,* Fall.

ROTH, GUENTHER 1963. *The Social Democrats in Imperial Germany.* New Jersey: Bedminster Press.

SCHUMPETER, JOSEPH A. 1951. *Imperialism and Social Classes.* Oxford: Blackwell.

SDS 1969. Black Panther Party Resolution. *New Left Review* (56), July–August.

STEEL, RONALD 1969. The Panthers. *New York Review of Books* **13** (4), 11 Sept.

TUMIN, MELVIN M., *et al.* 1958. *Desegregation.* Princeton, New Jersey: Princeton University Press.

VAN DEN BERGHE, PIERRE L. 1965. *South Africa: A Study in Conflict.* University of California Press.

VAN DEN BERGHE, PIERRE L. 1967. *Race and Racism.* New York: Wiley.

WAGLEY, CHARLES (ed.) 1963. *Race and Class in Rural Brazil.* UNESCO.

WILSON, JAMES Q. 1965. The Negro in Politics. *Daedalus*, Fall.

JOHN R. LAMBERT

Race Relations: the Role of the Police[1]

In 1967 the Commissioner of Police for the Metropolis wrote of
'the deteriorating background to the pattern of police and immigrant relations during the last six months'.[2] In April of that year the
National Council for Civil Liberties reported that in the Harrow
Road area of London 'there can be no doubt that the confidence
between police and the immigrant population is almost nonexistent'.[3] In July of that year the Home Office issued a circular
recommending that police forces in areas of significant immigration
appoint Liaison Officers.[4] A Community Relations Department has
been established at Scotland Yard to establish some kind of dia-
logue with immigrant communities and to coordinate the work of
the Metropolitan Liaison Officers. Complaints against the police
can be something of a measure of conflict: the rate of complaints
by coloured immigrants in the Metropolitan Police area exceeded
those made by the white majority by three to two. Although only
2·5 per cent of the complaints from coloured citizens are 'sub-
stantiated' by the current police investigatory system (as against
8·8 per cent for white complainants), it must be acknowledged that
this is an area where the sense of grievance, not its justification, is
the true measure of relationship. The claim that many of these
complaints are trivial puts a definition on them that is made by the
police themselves and may conceal a real sense of lost confidence.
The 1967 Campaign Against Racial Discrimination Report (CARD
1967) described in some detail five complaints of police brutality;
the recent television programme 'Cause for Concern'[5] explored
some serious cases where grave injustice was shown to have occurred. Whether such cases were 'typical' – either of complaints or
of police behaviour – is rather beside the point, as is the 'typicality'

73

of the very few officers who have had to be moved from their regular areas because of their being the subject of frequent complaints. A prerequisite of good policing, as is frequently noted, is 'good' relations between police and community. 'Good' in this situation means each actor in the relationship sharing a definition of 'proper' police action and 'proper' citizen behaviour: each must have a shared expectation of behaviour that allows for trust and confidence; each must be able to predict with reasonable certainty how the other will behave in a given situation.

A few memorable cases, however a-typical, will undermine positive expectations. Unless police and citizen share this definition of 'a-typicality', conflict rather than cooperation will characterize the relation. A few serious cases, and a mass of 'trivial' cases, suggest that from the citizen standpoint 'improper' police action is not incredible, but has become part of a negative expectation, a source of uncertainty, and a denial of confidence.

'Good' relations between police and public have never been easily won. From the first, Peel's new police had to school themselves to behaviour that was calculated to convince a number of critics that the new police idea was a good one. Problems persist with just those groups most uncertain about the central values of the society that the police serve, most uncertain about the extensive moral consensus upon which the police rely, or who meet with the exercise of the discretionary powers the police possess. Traditionally this has meant the working class, the urban poor, those most affected by crime and disorder, where peace-keeping is more direct a task than in the quietude of suburbia. It has also meant the young in conflict with the values of the parent generation. And in recent years the growth of a motoring public, with its particular offences and offenders, and a jurisdiction massively dependent upon selective discretionary prosecution by the police, has created a new source of uncertainty, if not hostility, towards the police. Some conflict and criticism are inevitable and of a long-standing nature. The remarkable reputation of the British police in solving these conflicts should not minimize the extent to which in the past the conflicts have been real and intense and required of the police purposive action at all levels to find a style of policing whose acceptance by the general population permits the complex tasks of law-enforcement and peace-keeping to be undertaken in a policed society rather than a police state.

What I want to suggest in this paper is that the growing number of complaints and the number of serious cases involving coloured citizens must be understood, not in terms of expressions by a few a-typical authoritarian policemen giving vent to their prejudices in individual acts of harassment and brutality, but 'normal' police action, behaviour, and attitudes moulded by custom and tradition both within the police system and in society at large.

Most of the reported cases of complaint derive from areas of London. This may be purely a communications distortion; such organizations as Campaign Against Racial Discrimination, the National Council for Civil Liberties, and the West Indian Standing Conference are London organizations and the national press reports their concerns. My own research was carried out in Birmingham: there was no evidence there of the same level and intensity of hostility between police and coloured citizens, but this is probably a matter of degree rather than of kind. What was observable in Birmingham was police officers sharing in widely held, openly expressed views about racial minorities that were derogatory and incapable of supporting the style of relationship necessary for 'good' police/community relations.

My starting-point for an examination of the police role is that suggested by the American scholars Reiss and Bordua:

'the police have as their fundamental task, the creation and maintenance of, and their participation in, external relationships. Indeed the central meaning of police authority itself is its significance as a mechanism for "managing" relationships' (Reiss and Bordua 1967).

Policing as an occupation requires that police officers must enter into relationships – or transact business – with all sorts and conditions of men. What a policeman does in such a setting depends on his perception of his 'client's' status and on whether the client is seen as complainant, complained of, or suspect. The policeman's view will be affected by his immediate occupational task – as CID man, patrol officer, traffic-man, vice-squad member, and so on. An independent variable in all these situations is what might be termed the 'citizen-attitude' of the policeman. In a given situation the client's own perception of the policeman and what role is justified, in so far as it affects his response to the policeman, will affect how the policeman perceives the client and interprets his behaviour. It is within this sort of framework that I want to explore the relationship between policeman and coloured citizen, and explain the conflicts that arise.

This relationship can be looked at from four points – or in terms of four parameters each of which points to the importance, described so well by Michael Banton (1964), of the interplay between the private and public roles the policeman has to play.

These four interrelated parameters are:

1 The legal role of the police and the extent to which law-enforcement is discretionary, not universalistic.
2 The varieties of transactions policemen and police forces are expected to perform as agents of the police service.
3 The nature of career structure and occupational specialization that occurs within the organized police force.
4 The nature of the 'police culture', which sets standards and norms for policemen as a group.

Clearly a full exploration of these is not possible at present: the lack of English studies of policing, and the very limited nature of my own research, mean a dependence on an American perspective and too much generalization. What follows is an attempt to point out how normal policing can be misunderstood by citizens who are newcomers, can appear as discriminatory and selective, and allows expression of individual attitudes and behaviours that derive from prejudice and stereotypes of a racist nature.

THE LEGAL ROLE

We use a variety of terms to describe what the police do. Most are imprecise and difficult to define in operational terms: keep the peace, maintain law and order, prevent crime, detect offenders, enforce the law. All such phrases involve an idea of service with authority. The legal philosophy of democratic society sees police activities as potentially threatening to individual liberty and implying a danger of arbitrary interference. Thus police forces enforce the law and are themselves bound by laws and regulations. The legal philosophy of democratic society also requires that all men shall be 'equal before the law', that all laws shall apply to all men, and that equal enforcement of the law shall be effected by the police. However, *full* enforcement is not possible (LaFave 1965); lawbreaking is so common that to investigate every infringement, to prosecute every known offender, would require police forces of a size, and involve expenditures of a scale, that would be impracticable and intolerable. So police forces of limited sizes and small budgets are obliged to undertake selective enforcement of some laws: the police possess, both as an organization and as individuals, considerable discretionary powers about how to organize, which crimes and criminals to prosecute, how to allocate what number of men to different law-enforcement tasks, and so on. The basis for selection rests broadly on two kinds of relationship – between the police force and the community, and between the individual officer and the client. The police force is subject to political pressures, formal and informal, organized and intermittent; police officers are pressured by their occupational norms derived from the Force, Division, Section, or Squad to which they belong.

Thus can be understood Michael Banton's important point that, for the police:

> 'the interplay between ends and means is much more complex than in most organizations. The efficiency of the police may, therefore, be less important than their responsiveness to the community they are required to serve' (Banton 1964: 105–6).

A contemporary American description of 'the policeman's art' makes the essential point:

> 'This consists in applying and enforcing a multitude of laws and ordinances in such a degree or proportion and in such manner that the greatest degree of protection will be secured. The degree

of enforcement and the method of application will vary with each neighborhood and community. There are no set rules, nor even general principles, to the policy to be applied. Each policeman must, in a sense, determine the standard to be set in the area for which he is responsible . . .' (Smith 1949).

But the police do have limits set for them by the legal system, since laws both bind and limit police operations and define what behaviours are the target for police action:

'Modern metropolitan police exist only in view of the fact that communities are legally organized. The problem of the external parameters of police operation and organization, in its broadest sense, inheres both in the nature of the urban community and in the nature of the legal system. Indeed the fundamental position of the police may be conceived as mediating between the two. On the one hand, the police are a fundamental representative of the legal system and a major source of raw material for it. On the other, the police adapt the universalistic demands of law to the structure of the locale by a wide variety of formal and informal devices' (Reiss and Bordua 1967).

This adaptive task of the police means, in effect, that customary morality, as perceived by the police or as interpreted to the police by 'political' pressures, tends to define law-enforcement. The police force thus tends to be an agency committed to establishing moral conformity; or in some instances achieving and maintaining social stability, by tolerating to a greater or lesser extent certain legal infractions – such as prostitution or some 'social' violence – if such do not threaten the sense of well-being of the dominant moral community. The use of discretion is the essential means whereby the police achieve what the legal philosophy of a democratic society adjures – selective, discretionary surveillance, enforcement, and prosecution of the law, in conformity with an existing pattern of relations.

The significance of discretion tends to be denied. The police assert that all they do is enforce the law, treat all alike, prosecute impartially. The ideal, legalistic definition of crime and policing matches quite well the classic story-book model of the great crime; discovery of offence, notification to police, detective skills applied to clues, trailing the suspect, prosecution in court. Such a pattern is unusual.

By far the most problematical police tasks are in relation to 'service' crimes – forbidden practices indulged in by willing 'victims' and 'offenders'. The police have to seek out wrongdoers; they serve no specific victim or complainant; they have to depend on their own devices to obtain information and evidence. Those interested in providing the opportunities for forbidden services are put into opposition to the police; to obtain evidence the police must participate in the 'vice', either directly by becoming witnesses, or by bargaining and buying off participants with a variety of gifts or threats or other tactics. Such actions lead to the development of specialist functions among technical police experts within the general police service. In such situations the police are forced into a game with very complicated and ever-changing rules. Often, as in relation to prostitution or drug-trafficking, the law is at its most ambiguous or uncertain – and the police are brought into conflict with groups who do not accept, and wish to challenge, the basis of the law in a particular set. The police, faced with a technically difficult task but required to act only within the law, are invited to operate illegally by virtue of their established position within the court whereby they can present a version of events with an *ex post facto* legality; innovation is concealed. The low status and marginality of typical offenders make it unlikely that the police version will be challenged.

Other kinds of discretionary enforcement apply to motoring offences and to offences of disorder and drunkenness. These more routine police operations give individual policemen considerable latitude in defining offence and offender. In practice, the process of interaction will determine outcome. Frequently the speeding motorist who is deferential and apologetic, the disorderly citizen who 'goes along quietly', and the drunk who can stutter out a plausible address and a sentence with something like 'sir' in it, will avoid prosecution. Abundant opportunities for a legalistic police to jam up the courts with speeders, and police cells with drunks, mean that a variety of organizational devices to control the zeal of police officers have to operate. The current concern about the war against crime, the police concern for a good 'clear-up' rate, mean that little value attaches to such kinds of work: a good arrest is one that involves a 'proper felon' – a thief of some kind – whose capture will inflate the success the police can claim in their law-enforcing mission.

Crime events of all kinds, and the various other incidents involving the police, are not evenly distributed throughout an area or city. As part of my Birmingham study, I took a census of a wide range of police events in a four-month period and considered where they occurred: these were reported crimes, police arrests of various kinds, and minor incidents to which the police were summoned. Of some 3,000 events in the Police Division studied – and the Division can be imagined as a triangle with its apex in the city centre and its base on the suburban southern boundary of the city – over 66 per cent occurred in the innermost wedge within one and a half miles of the centre, some 20 per cent in the middle zone, and about 15 per cent in the outer stretches of council estates and nice middle-class areas where lived nearly one-half of the Division's 225,000 residents. The event rate per 10,000 of population was six times greater in the inner area than in the outer ring. When the Division was considered as ten 'natural' areas, the rates ranged from a low 39 to a high 453. When divided into various kinds of event, the criss-cross of patterns was extensive. A large number of car-parks near the city centre, and a hostel for homeless men, inflated car thefts and arrests for drunkenness in the overall rate. Prostitution occurred in two distinct areas; violent disputes were more prevalent in some areas and almost nonexistent in others. This uneven distribution calls for, and reflects, an uneven distribution of police resources.

This uneven distribution of police resources means that police intervention and activity are greatest in those areas where concentrations of coloured families are highest. Although it is clear that in terms of comparative rates coloured immigrants are far from over-represented, immigrant areas, in Birmingham at any rate, are high-crime areas. In a number of situations there is significant contact between police and coloured citizens. The element of discretion in police work points to a particular style of intervention and relationship that is not merely an application of rules and laws, but depends on a very distinctly interpersonal interaction. Expectations of behaviour – crucially for the policeman a deference on the part of the 'client' to the policeman's authority, a showing of *respect* – rather than the law book or police regulations determine outcome.

VARIETIES OF TRANSACTIONS

The uniformed policeman in his day-to-day duties meets people who seek some advice from him in a wide variety of situations. Relatively infrequently is the person a suspect; the police intervention is more advisory than authoritarian. The uniformed policeman more often than not meets the complainant and victim not the suspect or offender. Other social duties – diverting traffic, crowd control, helping pedestrians, advising on crime prevention, road-safety liaison with schools, conveying messages from hospitals and for other bodies, visiting to assist the Fire Department at alarm calls – such actions as these, aspects of the traditional peace-keeping role that arise from the patrolling presence of the uniformed officer, ask of the police to engage in fairly straightforward 'helping' relationships.

Somewhat more ambiguous situations confront the uniformed officer when summoned to resolve a dispute – between families, neighbours, landlord and tenants, pub landlords and customers, café-owners and customers, etc. Commonly in such situations one party in the dispute makes a demand or bid for the backing of authority; the story is infrequently clear cut, both parties can justify a bid for police support. An appeal to the law is often unhelpful. The police are expected to resolve the conflict by finding a means of mediating between the disputants. Custom and tradition suggest a number of techniques. The most frequent was a plain denial of competence – 'This is not a police matter, nothing I can do, you must go elsewhere' – followed by a plea for calm and reason, sometimes supported by a warning about breaching the peace. The police task is to get the disputants to behave reasonably, the presence of an authoritarian stranger, a few words of advice, a warning, some reassurance, are all that is possible. The policeman's ultimate authority, his power of arrest, is here a threat rather than a reality; instances when it proves necessary to invite one of the disputants outside 'for a word' when an arrest for drunkenness or disorder in a public place can be effected exist, not only in folklore, but as a pragmatic response to necessity. Such would indicate a failure of 'reasonableness', requiring police to restructure the situation to allow a definition of 'offender' to apply in order to justify arrest.

As was suggested earlier, even in clear-cut cases of legal infringements – for the uniformed patrol officer or squad-car man typically in terms of motoring offences or drunk and disorderly behaviour – there is no automatic definition of the person as an 'arrestable' or 'prosecutable offender'. In the process of interaction, the offender's behaviour and attitude can determine whether he will be the subject of police process. How the offender responds to police authority, what *respect* he shows the individual policeman, will determine the action that is taken.

Policing for the uniformed officer is largely an ever-changing series of contacts demanding an individually directed response. A policeman, to be successful, must learn how to 'handle people'. This involves his being able to sum up a person very quickly and determine a suitable manner for that person, in that situation; he must have some expectations of the person's response, and mould his manner to attain some given end. At its simplest, this means that the policeman does not treat everyone the same: depending on his perception of class, status, occupation, education, bearing, etc., the policeman discriminates in his behaviour on the basis of a stereotype.

In his transactions with coloured citizens, the policeman has little experience on which to base his expectations. His 'given' stereotypes are predictable and largely derogatory. In Birmingham it seemed that police expectations of Asian immigrants were moulded by an uncertainty deriving from language barriers, so that suspicion rather than hostility shaped the relation. The number of officers with a grasp of the conversational dialects of the Asian immigrants is limited; the normal procedure is for the 'client' to involve a friend or relative as interpreter. This need to use interpreters does undoubtedly pose additional difficulties for the police in managing such relationships; opportunities of misunderstanding are multiplied as are demands on police sensitivity, intelligence, and patience. Such problems seem to have given the Asian citizens a reputation for deceitfulness and cunning, because of incidents where the police view was that the language barrier was being used to evade questioning or provide inadequate answers. It was sometimes suggested that, in his dealings with officials of any kind, it is almost customary for the Asian immigrant to presume an absolute corruptibility on the part of the official, which, though a useful and necessary (and accurate) presumption to make in the homeland, can only appear as devious and dishonest to the fundamentally incorruptible British bobby.

With the West Indian – although language difficulties may well be underestimated – police relations seemed moulded by expectations of excitability and 'arrogance'. Excitability is the opposite of 'coming along quietly'; 'arrogance' is the opposite of showing respect, a failure to defer to police authority. The police use of discretion requires that police authority is acknowledged as valid but that its ultimate sanction – arrest – is something of a last resort. Like any servant the policeman is happiest when requested, he resents demands. In his relationships with citizens he wants to keep open a number of lines for action – he wants some freedom in defining roles for himself and the client – and this is easier with a compliant response, a cooperative manner, an acceptance of discussion and advice. The man who declines to play the game by these, the policeman's, rules is a challenge. He denies the policeman a favoured role situation and forces him into a formal, rule-bound, nondiscretionary relationship. The citizen who asserts his rights is difficult because what a policeman needs to do is to persuade and appease and guide. The 'arrogance' imputed to the West Indian prevents 'normal' communication and pushes the policeman back upon his authority, – to demanding rather than commanding respect, – from which stems hostility. An observed example may illustrate this:

D

'At about 3 a.m. on a Friday morning, an area car was summoned to the help of a patrolling officer in Balsall Heath. He had been called to a café in the area to investigate some "trouble" involving four young West Indian men and a local 17-year-old English girl. When he got there he found the party leaving in a van; he stopped them and questioned them. The girl complained that she was being forced to go with one of the men against her will. As she was clearly very upset, the policeman thought that a kerbside discussion was inappropriate and suggested that they all go to the police station.

At the station, the four men were sat down at a table and the girl was asked to explain the situation. The girl's story was that she had previously been going out with one of the men but had broken the relationship. They had met again that evening and he had tried to persuade her against her will to go with him. He had made her get into his van, her protests and complaints having no effect. When she had finished her story, the man concerned suggested quite vehemently that the police should not just listen to her story but only judge after hearing his version. One of the policemen, clearly incensed by the man's manner, went up to him and almost shouted, "Who do you think you're talking like that to? You'd better show more respect. Don't talk to a policeman like that."

The West Indian replied with equal fervour: "You're not going to frighten me like that. Don't think you can beat me up in a police station and get away with it."

There followed an angry and incoherent exchange during which both men spoke at once and which ended abruptly with the West Indian saying: "Why pick on me for this, you only do so because I'm black." "Oh!" replied the policeman, "thanks for telling me, I hadn't noticed." Thereafter any reasonable discussion was impossible. Truculently the West Indian asserted, "I won't say anything except to a solicitor." A few more questions were directed at the girl. It seemed very clear that no offences had been committed; this was a dispute in which the girl found herself in an unwelcome situation from which she was unable to extricate herself and so the police were involved. The manner adopted by the parties prevented "normal" advice and discussion: it swiftly floundered in resentment and recrimination. Names and addresses were taken, the vehicle checked for licence, tax, and insurance, and the parties sent home. Angered by the "arrogance" of the West Indian, a policeman remarked, "In a few years time they'll be ordering us about and telling *us* what to do." '

Such an incident points up the kinds of tensions that are fairly typical of contact between black citizen and white policeman. Nothing in a policeman's training and experience teaches him how to manage a relationship with a person who denies him the traditional and customary police role. All he has to rely on are his 'citizen attitudes' – derogatory, and prejudiced, if not racist. The various techniques of bonhomie or bombast, or the stylized deference the police adopt in relation to 'better-class' whites, that suffice for the traditional clientele are irrelevant in the new situation. In addition, the black citizen and the black community will not necessarily share a view of the police held by any white class or white community; indeed, their experience of police in the homeland may mean that they are likely to have an expectation of police violence or hostility. The components of the relationship – shared expectations of uncertainty and unpredictability – mean that distance, hostility, and fear are inevitable. The relation can, on Cohen's definition, be characterized by 'disorganization' (Cohen 1966). The police have not learned, or acquired, techniques whereby they can perform their conflict-reducing tasks in relating to members of racial minorities.

POLICE ORGANIZATIONS

By far the majority of contacts between police and coloured citizens involve uniformed officers in situations that carry no immediate definition of 'suspect', 'offence', or 'offender'. The attitudes and beliefs derived from such contacts, characterized, as I believe them to be, by uncertainty, suspicion, and hostility, will affect the credibility attached to the widely current complaints. The most serious of these will tend to derive from contacts between non-uniformed specialist CID or plain-clothes 'vice-squad' police and coloured citizens in situations where the definition of 'criminal' or 'offender' does apply, at any rate as far as the police are concerned. A perspective on this aspect of policing is important.

The vast majority of reported crimes are not amenable to much detective work. All the CID can do is to hold on to cases in the hope that someone caught red-handed in some crime will admit his part in a series of other offences to be taken into consideration by the court. Forty-four per cent of the recorded 'clear-up' rate for crimes in the Birmingham survey was attributable to talkative offenders rather than the skills of detectives. In fact, routine CID work is highly administrative; it involves the effective processing of offenders caught by uniformed patrolmen in such a way as to reveal the maximum number of offences. The crime rate is slightly inflated as a result of this process. Crimes that were never reported are admitted by offenders, and one offence can reveal others, as when a teenage fight revealed a series of sexual misdemeanours that would otherwise never have been recorded. Quite unlike the Crime Squad, which handles highly skilled, organized, technically complex investigations of major crimes, the local CID men have an impossible task, with huge case-loads of unsolvable crimes. Yet their work provides the only measure of success used by the police – the clear-up rate.

The complete operation of policing suffers by this distortion. The necessity for a good clear-up rate, makes the CID depend on effective criminal-catching operations; the uniformed patrol services the CID with suspects – this is what constitutes 'good' police work. A policeman knows that his success within the force will depend on his record of good arrests – that is, of persons who contribute to a good clear-up rate. So uniformed police tend not to attach much value to many of the advising/helping 'service' tasks they are asked to perform; in the main they are on the look-out for suspects. This is not a detective function so much as a search for persons who can be defined as offenders, who merit police attention.

Police organization serves to differentially associate police officers with society at points where it is more likely that an excess of definitions favourable to 'offender' will be obtained. Anyone definable as a 'suspect' will be approached in a certain way to see if the definition will stick; police discriminate against those who look guilty. And police organization and culture provide a set of definitions of those who look guilty: by definition, anyone who has been in 'trouble' before is scrutinized continually, and is liable to be brought in or approached for questioning; the police discriminate against those known to have been guilty in the past.

In so far as 'problem areas' are those where opportunities for 'offender-labelling' abound – and problem areas are coloured areas – the definition of 'suspect' will be generously applied in those areas.

The plain-clothes branch, or vice-squad CID, are in a particularly difficult spot; they start with suspects, observed offenders, and are in search of court-proof evidence that will convict them. They operate in areas where they must seek to conceal their identity, for typically the situations where the infringements are occurring involve groups of people suspicious of outsiders who threaten their invisibility. The police need to involve informers, and have contacts and influence with participants. They are thus forced into a highly ambiguous relationship with wrongdoers in an attempt to create a structure of events that will permit a raid, evidence, and court conviction. The knowledge that their version of events will be believed in court rather than anyone else's creates many opportunities for extra-legal police work.

It is a major task for police management to provide sufficient controls on police malpractices in the area of plain-clothes work. The demands of 'production' and success can overcome these controls and lead to situations such as those described in the Sheffield scandal of a few years ago (Home Office 1963). A more recent case found a high-court judge dismissing a case where a local CID had negotiated a deal with a member of a criminal gang whereby he and his fellows were caught in the act, but only the fellows were prosecuted. Disputes about planted evidence in drug offences, raids without warrants or on warrants granted too cursorily, the case of the car keys planted on the complainants whose story was shown in 'Cause for Concern'[6] – these suggest what happens when police organization fails to give adequate directives and supervision to policemen in action. The secretive and somewhat elitist position of plain-clothes branches within police forces, combined with a tradition of idiosyncratic and highly individualistic operations, adds to the problems.

The managerial position of senior police officers in relation to the uniformed branch is similarly problematical. The organizational style – uniforms with polished buttons, numbers, ranks, parades, and salutes – suggests a formally disciplined force. But policing, as I suggested, cannot be squeezed into a book of formal regulations. What tends to happen, I believe, is that *within* the force there is great stress on formal rules and relations, a dependence upon routine: this does not extend beyond the station house. Traditional managing by senior police has been in terms of supervision once a case is produced by the individual officer. The problem for the police is to extend this managerial supervision to the decision about how and whether a person or incident becomes a 'case'. Nothing in police organizational style suggests the extent of discretionary authority wielded by the police officer. Indeed, discretion tends to be denied. Far from wielding a force with a coherent, coordinated, policy-directed enterprise, demands of routine and regimentation paradoxically permit highly individualistic operations. On the street, a policeman is on his own; advice and direction come not from senior managerial officers but from his immediate colleagues and from the norms and values operating in a 'police culture'.

THE 'POLICE CULTURE'

Police training does little to reflect what I have suggested is the fundamental task of the police, that of managing relationships. Large chunks of law, first aid, and some ancillary lectures on social studies are not very relevant to the routine tasks, which are learned primarily from respected older officers. The police group becomes important in moulding attitudes and behaviour. The current emphasis on criminal-catching and the devaluation of 'service' tasks within the police culture reflects the growing sense of 'professionalism' claimed by the police. Law-enforcement officers do not want to be thought of as 'social workers'. Only sociologists, I suspect, are held in lower esteem in police circles. Yet the traditional demands remain to occupy a great deal of a policeman's time. The decline in value of this kind of work can be related to the fact that it is no longer true that a policeman polices his own community. Traditional practices allow some officers to recognize categories of persons in need of help. But this is declining with the changing nature of the policeman's identification with the community he polices.

It is valuable to note Michael Banton's remark that

'Policemen's actions are governed by morality more than law . . . and in conflict morality wins. They prefer to persuade rather than prosecute . . . they see the office vested with moral authority as well as legal power' (Banton 1964).

This is why the influence of a policeman's private roles upon how he performs his public role is so important. The success of the village constable, and the esteem in which he was held (even allowing for nostalgic distortion), derived from his being perceived as a person not a professional, and from his enforcing standards accepted by the community. Traditionally, even in the city, police were recruited locally; they were not severed from their background; it was possible for the policeman, usually a resident of a station house in the vicinity, to be known as more than just a policeman. The growth of the police profession, a tendency for colonies of police houses to develop in certain neighbourhoods, the growing social and area mobility of the aspiring middle class with whom the policeman identifies, have removed the policeman from the opportunity to have the old style of links in the community he serves. So currently the successful policeman, detective or uniformed, lives somewhere other than where he works – he is a visitor to the area. This is particularly true of those areas where crime and disorder are most frequent and where the police are in frequent intervention. But the policeman still enforces conventional morality as much as the law, still has discretionary powers to interpret the law for the community he polices. Inevitably the suburban mores and those of the heterogeneous central residential area are in conflict. A policeman has only limited contact with his clients; he sees them as a partial social category: slum-dweller, social problem, misfit, criminal, drug-taker, pimp. He is himself seen as a social category. His most pressing problems as a professional are in relation to areas and neighbourhoods in which he is viewed as an 'outsider'.

This lack of identification and acceptance in areas where the need is for a relationship based on confidence and trust poses problems for men who have to spend a considerable amount of their working-time so placed. The policeman looks for contacts and friends with whom the sense of isolation is minimized; one should not underestimate the extent to which boredom is a problem for the routine patrolling officer, so that the friendly café-owner with a warm back-room, the local tolerated after-hours pub, the factory watchman with teapot and radio, become essential friends. In so far as regulations forbid such practices, the loyalty of the group in support of these common 'easing' techniques is required and maintained (see Cain 1969).

Another problem to be overcome is the danger inherent in much police work: a stress of toughness, a readiness for self-defence, and a manner in uncertain relationships that will quickly establish personal superiority and deter aggression – the 'right' language, verbal assault, is an important technique as is a threat of the use of force.

The police are subject to insults; offenders caught in the act are sometimes perverse in their refusal to admit additional offences; the instructions given to the police by judges' rules and senior officers are unclear; the pressure to produce results is great; the knowledge that one's word in court is virtually unimpeachable when the offender more likely than not has a record, or can be shown to have a stake in discrediting the officer: these, in the context of a strong shared loyalty within an organization whose command structure is not always clear, coherent, and consistent, and where formal adherence to rules is linked to an informal avoidance of their declared intentions, provide a setting in which to understand the view of the ex-policeman interviewed on 'Cause for Concern':

'Well, there is this sort of hard man cult which exists among the lower ranks and this requires a young man to prove himself in many ways. Mainly it requires him to prove himself by the number of arrests he makes . . . the coloured man is not as fully aware of his rights as a white man would be and on this assumption I suppose he would be more vulnerable. But I think generally that the prejudice that exists would make him more vulnerable. . . . It's very difficult to preserve any individual views that one might have had at the outset . . . you get carried along with the tide. Very difficult. . . It would have been out of the question [to object], I would have been socially unacceptable within the police force.'[7]

The policeman, like most white people, has little or no understanding of the 'immigrant community'. To the extent that, as an official, he possesses a view of 'integration', he is likely to share the 'suppressive' version that views the coloured immigrant as a welfare problem whose customs need modification. For the policeman, the entrepreneurial activities of a minority of immigrants in the café/club/brothel environment of the problem area will reinforce this view. The problem of the area comes to be seen as 'caused' by the most visible 'problem' group whose encroachment into the other areas is seen as a threat or a danger.

John Rex (Rex and Moore 1967) has described how processes within the housing market provide the framework of the race-relations problem in Birmingham. A second-class housing system tends to segregate a problem area that includes 'various ethnic communities, transitional people awaiting rehousing and isolates and deviants of all sorts'. Competition for limited housing of good quality means that social prejudice is functional for those concerned to maintain a position of privilege in the class struggle over housing. This explains the widespread prejudice and the subtle and unsubtle forms of discrimination it produces. Most concerned with maintaining the position are the middle-class group and the aspiring middle class who have achieved the move from zone of transition to suburbia: as citizens, policemen are recent movers on these terms.

'Professional' attitudes and 'citizen' attitudes thus tend to complement each other, making explicable the view of the 'Cause for Concern' ex-policeman that 'the colour prejudice is virtually absolute. In other words it extends probably ninety-nine per cent'.[8]

I have attempted to provide a broad perspective on the police function in urban areas that can suggest how and why the normal and traditional police practices are increasingly irrelevant for policing the kind of urban society growing in our cities, and are likely to promote rather than reduce conflict among such communities and between the segments of those communities. I do not mean to suggest that police practices are misunderstood by unsophisticated citizens with a different experience of police systems, although there is a tendency on the part of officials to see the problem merely as one of communications. What I wish to stress is that the new communities in our cities make new demands on police services, as on other agencies and institutions. Currently, the traditional ways and means of policing are proving unsatisfactory in solving new problems. Improved communications without a preparedness on the part of the police to recognize and act upon demands for change, most crucially at the level of the uniformed and detective constable on the beat, will only increase dissatisfactions not reduce or resolve them.

Uncertainties and conflicts in role and performance that are not resolved by police organization will make individual policemen rely on their individual perception of person, community, and need. Traditionally this was a functional reliance, because the policeman understood and lived with his own community. Now his individual attitudes are those of a society increasingly anxious, fearful, and resentful of coloured racial minorities.

How important is this for the future of race relations: is the police role peripheral or central to the pattern that will unfold in the coming years? Here we must return to an idea quoted at the outset of this paper:

'. . . the police are a fundamental representative of the legal system, and a major source of raw material for it' (Reiss and Bordua 1967).

As representatives of the legal system, as a uniformed visible presence, as the only agency at work twenty-four hours a day seven days a week, the police are important symbols of authority in the community. As such, they are representative of more than just the police service, they stand for 'official endeavour' in a community. Police tend to be asked to do much more than enforce the law: they are asked to help families in need, search for runaway daughters and truanting children, restrain and admonish drinking fathers and careless mothers, berate inattentive landlords, search out peeping toms, make noisy parties quiet, complain about bad street lights and crumbling pavements, damaged kiosks, and gipsies; they are expected to mind those wounded in accidents in street and home, and to help those affected by fires and illness. Most of the corporal works of mercy are a task for the police, and in so far as they involve contact with those in distress and in need, and among those confused and uncertain about their rights and duties, whether a policeman cares or is seen to care, or can be trusted rather than feared, can be expected to affect a persons' view of whether society cares.

As a 'major source of raw material' for the legal system, the police wield considerable power. The current bouts of complaint point to two kinds of malpractice: use of power when not justified, non-use of power when it was justified. In the long run, complaints that police treat offences against coloured citizens less carefully, or that offences by coloured citizens are not investigated because of the difficulties the police have in making inquiries, may prove most corrosive to the confidence that must exist as a precondition of the police functioning at all.

Thus the kind of race relations practised by the police is of great importance. Policing needs a basic shared understanding of the police role communicated between policeman and citizen, police force and community. Traditionally, I believe the police to have been remarkably successful in winning the confidence and trust of the public. The extensive – some would say extraordinary – powers possessed by the police, and the assumption that the police can be expected to use them reasonably, are in contrast with the situation in the United States. The lack of hostility between police and the white community in this country is remarkable and valuable; but it is also, ironically, a problem in relations between police and the coloured community.

In discussing my research, in particular that part which suggests the scope that exists for police to initiate a new kind of relationship on which sound police practice could be based, with senior police officers, it was stressed to me that the police cannot afford to run ahead of public opinion. It was stressed how real are the local pressures – expressed formally and informally – within which policing has to be organized. Senior officers are aware of the 'normal' prejudices of police officers. I believe they underestimate the extent to which 'citizen' attitudes mould occupational behaviour. They are also aware of the murmurs and shouts of support for Powell-type arguments – both among the ranks of policemen and among those elements in communities who appeal for police action. They are sensitive about seeming to do too much that is positive – they do not want to promote conflict from a quarter that represents their traditional allies. 'Of course if we did what the [white] community *really* wanted . . .' and the sentence did not need completing.

This kind of anxiety shows how the police force is caught in the race-relations controversy. Technically, they are faced with considerable difficulties; politically, the pressures are such that they cannot do more than make a token stab at their solution – by labelling some officers 'Liaison Officers', by having some lectures at training school, by employing one or two coloured policemen. The anxiety about the relationship with the community to which traditionally they respond is not matched by anxiety about the current relationship with the new groups and communities for which policing is a more direct concern than many others. The convenient rationalization of a 'rotten apples' hypothesis is not, as I have tried to show, an adequate diagnosis of the existing situation.

The unwillingness to respond to new demands from the communities of coloured citizens, and the other side of that coin, the

willingness to respond to part of the total community, is the story
of relations between black citizen and white policeman in America.
As Herman Goldstein pointed out recently:

> 'There is considerable public opposition to the kind of efforts
> that go into programmes designed to improve relationships with
> minority groups . . . . In some cities . . . the programmes have
> been characterized as "molly-coddling" and are therefore sub-
> ject to attack on the broad grounds that a firmer position is called
> for on the part of the police in their relationships with the com-
> munity. On the other hand, police chiefs have been subject to
> direct criticism for example, for taking the initiative in attempt-
> ing to recruit Negro police officers. . . . The net result has been
> that most police chiefs, sensitive to the source of their power,
> have grown reluctant to extend themselves beyond the point at
> which they are assured of support by the community as a whole,
> and, more especially, by those to whom they are directly respon-
> sible . . . the impression I have is that many police admini-
> strators feel they have gone about as far as they can go without
> endangering their own relationships with the larger community'
> (Goldstein 1968).

The police chief in San Francisco was reported not many years
ago as saying:

> 'The police administrator to-day must understand that the
> desired relationship between the police and the public can be
> obtained only by a deliberate and calculated effort. It cannot be
> expected to develop by chance or at random, as in the past.'

Significantly he added that it was not a statement he would have
made five years earlier (Radelet 1966).

Unfortunately such a statement is more than five years too late in
the States: one only hopes that English police administrators looking across the Atlantic will not be seduced by computerized pro-
gramming of police patrols and other exciting technological devices
and advances, but will look at the effects of failing to reach a
relationship with minority groups in urban areas based even on a
minimum of trust and confidence, and at efforts now being made to

bridge the gap. To dismiss the complaints of coloured citizens as deriving from a handful of militants and extremists concerned to whip up trouble, – or to accept 'arrogance' as a characteristic chip West Indians wear on their shoulders, and adopt a 'business-as-usual' approach, ignores the fundamental prerequisites of policing. What the police have to learn to do – individual officers and the police service – is to relate to coloured citizens in ways that enable their essential tasks of public service – the prevention of crime, the reduction of social conflicts, the maintenance of social order, the creation of an aura of confidence and stability – to be performed effectively. Race *relations*, so defined is a prerequisite of good policing.

As I was preparing this paper, *New Society* published an article by Seymour Lipset, 'The Politics of the Police', which explores how the class orientation of the police as a group creates a sense of alienation and right-wing radicalism morally outraged at the conspiratorial corrupters of American society, i.e. minorities and leftist radicals. The opening remarks of that article provide an appropriate end-piece to this paper:

> 'Ortega y Gasset predicted in his book, *The Revolt of the Masses*, published in 1930, that free societies would come to fear their police. He argued that those who rely on the police to maintain order are foolish if they imagine that the police "are always going to be content to preserve . . . order (as defined by government) . . . inevitably (the police) will end by themselves defining and deciding on the order they are going to impose – which, naturally, will be that which suits them best"' (Lipset 1969).

There are elements of just that fear in the current hostility and conflict in relations between coloured citizens and their police.

Notes

1 This paper derives from some research carried out under the auspices of the Survey of Race Relations in Britain in Birmingham in 1966–7. The full research report, with the title *Crime, Police, and Race*

Relations, is to be published by the Oxford University Press for the Institute of Race Relations in 1970.
2 *The Job* (the newspaper for Metropolitan Police Officers) in the editorial 'Man to Man', 8 December 1967.
3 See *The Guardian,* 29 April 1967.
4 Home Office Letter to all Chief Constables dated 7 July 1967, 'The Police and Coloured Communities'.
5 'Equal Before the Law' a programme in the BBC 1 TV series 'Cause for Concern' screened 9 August 1968. The quotations cited later in this paper are taken from a transcript of part of this programme which was printed in *The Black Dwarf,* 14 August 1968.
6 Ibid.
7 Ibid.
8 Ibid.

References

BANTON, MICHAEL 1964. *The Policeman in the Community.* London: Tavistock Publications; New York: Basic Books.

CAIN, MAUREEN 1969. *Conflict and its Solution: an examination of an urban and rural police division,* esp. pp. 65, 94–104, 227–34, University of London Ph.D. Thesis. To be published 1970 by Routledge as *Policeman in Focus.*

COHEN, ALBERT K. 1966. *Deviance and Control.* New Jersey: Prentice Hall.

CAMPAIGN AGAINST RACIAL DISCRIMINATION 1967. *Report on Racial Discrimination.* London (mimeographed).

GOLDSTEIN, HERMAN 1968. The Role of the Police, paper read at the 14th National Institute for Police-Community Relations, Michigan State University, Lansing, USA.

HOME OFFICE 1963. *Sheffield Police Appeal Inquiry.* Cmnd. 2176. London: HMSO.

LA FAVE, WAYNE 1965. *Arrest: The Decision to Take a Suspect into Custody.* Boston: Little, Brown.

LIPSET, SEYMOUR 1969. The Politics of the Police. *New Society,* 6 March.

RADELET, LOUIS 1966. Implications of Professionalism in Law Enforcement for Police and Community Relations. *Police,* 10 June 1967.

REISS, A. & BORDUA, D. 1967. Environment and Organization: A Perspective on the Police. In Bordua, D. (ed.), *The Police: six sociological essays.* New York and London: Wiley.

REX, JOHN, & MOORE, ROBERT 1967. *Race, Community, and Conflict:
a Study of Sparkbrook*. London: Oxford University Press for the
Institute of Race Relations.
SMITH, BRUCE 1949. *Police Systems in the United States*. New York:
Harper.

SHEILA ALLEN

Immigrants or Workers

The situation in which coloured immigrants to this country find themselves, when at work, is similar in many respects to that of white workers. They become part of an industrial structure, employed largely in highly organized industrial units, where it is not within their control to determine the conditions of work and payment, though negotiations by their representatives may be a recognized part of the industrial-relations machinery. The hierarchical nature of the organization may mean they have little contact with anyone above the first-line supervisor and only a general idea of how the firm is run. Equally, the union is represented to them by the local officials and the officers within their own workshop or factory. National or regional policies may be imperfectly understood and officials at these levels unknown. The relationship between the local union and local managements may be seen as highly idiosyncratic and represented in terms of personal reputation and a series of anecdotes based on past experience. The structure of the situation in which people work is not immediately apparent to them. Any particular group of workers operates within a context of complex and interacting forces. It is important when attempting to assess the significance of empirical data to locate them within this context.

This paper describes an attempt to analyse some aspects of such a situation. It illustrates the present shortcomings of macro-social theory, the difficulties of crossing, in a meaningful way, the boundaries of specializations within sociology itself, and the substantive problems of research into a politically grounded and policy-oriented field.

THE THEORETICAL APPROACH

The tendency to adopt an approach that seeks to analyse inter-ethnic relations in terms of phases of absorption is still prevalent in the sociology of race relations. Two recent studies of employment (Patterson 1968; Wright 1968) attempt to use indices of immigrant absorption in British industry. This approach is rejected on a number of grounds. Whatever the definition used of the particular terms involved, it is virtually impossible to escape from the suggestion that these phases form part of a progression towards a non-conflictual generally acceptable state of inter-ethnic relations, normatively oriented towards some system of common values. This type of approach is heavily influenced by the processes assumed to have taken place during European immigration to the United States in the nineteenth and early twentieth centuries. Careful examination by American sociologists and psychologists of minority–majority relationships has shown these processes to be far more complex, and the instances of acceptance by the majority of minority group members on an equal status footing to continue to be more infrequent, than the 'phases of absorption' thesis would lead us to expect.[1] Moreover, these phases have rarely been considered to apply to relations involving American Negroes or Indians or, latterly, Puerto Ricans. That is they are properly limited if not to ethnically homogeneous at least to 'racially' homogeneous populations. The limitations exhibited by this conceptual framework when viewed as sociological propositions about relationships within a racially mixed, but white-dominated, society make it untenable theoretically and empirically invalid. This is not to say that in some situations forms of interaction do not exist, even at the present time, in which race is irrelevant. In such instances the last stage of the phase of absorption has already been reached, but this tells us nothing about the emerging relationships between racial groups in Britain. There is no inevitable progression, and processes of absorption are, as previous historical instances have shown, reversible. In fact, one can point to the situation in Britain in which long-established coloureds have during the past two decades become 'immigrants'.

Students of race relations tend to deal with specific situations using *ad hoc* concepts and substantially neglect to relate these to propositions and theories about the macro-structures. This general neglect is due among other reasons to the concern with immediate practical problems, the traditional emphasis on attitudes and the dynamics of prejudice and questions of acculturation, rather than a consideration of crucial elements of the social structures within which the specific situation is located. Conversely, sociologists who concern themselves with the more general overall structure tend to ignore race or colour as a factor in political and economic relations. At most, it is introduced as a 'complicating' or 'distorting' element in the 'normal' pattern of relationships. Our problem was to attempt to bridge this gap by considering the specific situation of coloured immigrant workers in Bradford within the context of the overall industrial structure. The system of social, political, and economic domination is relevant to the social relationships within a particular labour market or workplace, whatever the ethnic composition of the work-force. We did not, therefore, focus on colour as a major explanatory variable, but tried to relate the dimension of ethnicity or colour systematically to the totality of the social process.[2]

The views and practices of employers, the statements and activities of trade unionists, and the attitudes and behaviour of coloured immigrant workers were analysed in these terms. The information was frequently contradictory. The groups gave conflicting interpretations of some situations, and individuals within all the groups indicated discrepancies of attitude on particular points.

THE LOCAL SITUATION

Bradford industry appears to have employed coloured migrants with little or no friction in a variety of industries and services.[3] The majority are Pakistanis, with Indians and West Indians forming a much smaller proportion of the work-force.[4] Hypotheses and generalizations in race-relations research based on notions of integration did not accord with the reality of the Pakistanis' position.

In terms of religion and customs affecting family patterns, their beliefs and practices did not conform to the majority way of life found in Bradford. A secularized Christianity and the primacy of the nuclear family pattern of obligations between husband and wife and parents and children taken as the norm differs markedly from a strict observance of Islam and the primacy of male relationships whether between brothers, or between father and sons. In addition, the male migrants were oriented towards raising the standard of living of themselves and their dependants in relation to Pakistan rather than Britain.

When we began our research little was known about the employment situation of the coloured migrant workers.[5] Estimates of numbers, their distribution within and between industries, their relations at work, their attitudes to unions and to the conditions in which they worked, the experience of recruitment, and many other basic facts were not available. To test any of the sociological generalizations and to answer any of the policy questions these basic facts had to be collected.

It was pertinent that in Bradford it was widely believed at the time we began our work that no race problem existed and that Bradford was setting an example to other areas in its management of the race situation.[6] There had been no race violence, housing problems were not so acute an area of dissension as in, for instance, Birmingham and parts of London, and in education the authority had devised and put into operation a policy with which to contain the problem. Attitudes to the local race situation in which the research was to be carried out were by no means static.[7] Some indication of official opinion was the advice we were given to concentrate on real social problems in the city because there was no problem with 'our immigrants', who were happy and should be kept so.[8] Our attempts to get basic figures were in fact effectively blocked in this instance. Fortunately this lack of cooperation was the exception for larger undertakings, which were willing in different degrees to furnish at least basic information.

In the initial stages of our research our contacts with coloured immigrant groups and organizations were gradually built up in a generally favourable situation. However, by the time we came to carry out our interviewing of the sample of coloured immigrant workers in the summer of 1967 this situation had changed considerably, so that the lines between black and white were becoming more overtly and sharply drawn. We had already decided to use, in so far as it was possible, interviewers from the same ethnic group as the interviewees. This policy proved to be not only desirable, as we had assumed, but a necessity in the circumstances.[9]

EMPLOYMENT AS THE FOCUS

The existence within one local area of groups of workers, ethnically distinct and recently arrived from economically dependent and less industrialized areas of the world, to work among, if not alongside, the local population provided an opportunity almost unique in Britain for exploring some of the generalizations made in industrial sociology as well as in race relations. No study existed of the situation in which Pakistanis predominated as the main coloured immigrant labour force within the area and in which they were heavily concentrated in some industries and grades.[10]

The choice of employment as the major focus of our study was also based on the proposition that allocation within the industrial and occupational structure is closely related to allocation within the overall stratification system. It appeared to us that other questions – of housing, education, and to some extent forms of inter-ethnic relationships in the wider social sense – are dependent to a large degree on the present and future opportunities in employment. It is not suggested that the life-chances of present coloured immigrants and those of their children are mechanically determined by the jobs they obtain, nor that random allocation throughout the occupational structure would necessarily lead to some form of total social acceptance. But the relation between occupation and income level is sufficiently close to make employment patterns crucial in the setting of life-styles, including for instance access to certain educational opportunities and residential areas. In so far as any association between colour and particular (low) occupational levels is emerging the possibility of associating colour and low class position is reinforced.[11] The pressures towards social separation and ethnic isolation are consequential on job allocation in terms of ethnic group membership. Seen in relation to more general developments within the employment structure towards white-collar occupations and away from heavy manual work, Bob Hepple comments 'The danger is that coloured workers will find themselves relegated, by reason of discrimination, to the declining activity of manual labour' (Hepple 1968:62). Further, in so far as automation replaces some of the lower grades of manual work, 'this could result in a growing pool of unemployed, unskilled and semi-skilled coloured labour' (Hepple 1968:63). Relations between workers at these levels will be such that economic competition will become racial conflict.

The basic question that faced us in structuring our research was to what extent we were dealing with a situation located within the assumptions and procedures of industrial sociology and how far and in what ways we should use the existing framework and concerns of race-relations research. In brief, were we dealing with immigrants or workers? What emphasis should we give, for instance, to ethnic origins, differences in colour, and questions of language, what emphasis to the prevailing socio-economic structure of the industrial community with which we were concerned? Our decision on this emphasis affected who we should interview and the questions we would ask, that is the kind of factual data we should collect. We gave initially, and therefore continuously, more weight to the industrial structure within which interracial relations were developing.

Few industrial sociologists have considered the implications of ethnic stratification. Textbooks on industrial sociology lack in general any discussion of this phenomenon in relation either to the industrial structure itself or its effects on the wider society. Despite the historical importance of the black element in the labour force of the United States, relatively little attention has been paid to it until very recently in analysing the development of the industrial structure. On the whole, industrial sociologists have given inadequate attention to the part played by ethnicity factors in industrial organization and structure. Those concerned with race have focused on discrimination in employment but have rarely investigated systematically the relationship of discriminatory practices to the overall industrial-relations situation.[12] Consequently, understanding and explanation of significant areas of social relations still remain largely unattempted.[13]

Immigrant labour forces have been studied, but usually in relation to their transition to dominant group norms with their peculiarities of behaviour treated as temporary adjustments to particular situations. Relatively little work exists even in this area in relation to Britain and almost no attention has been paid in Britain by industrial sociologists to the immigrant nature of workforces and the development of industrial relations within the context of ethnic subgroupings.[14] In the present case a long-term study of the situation is necessary in order that the variables of immigrant and colour can be systematically related to the effects of changes in technical and commercial organization, the demand and supply of labour, and shifts in the power relationships within industries. In this way the race-relations situation can be seen in terms of the ongoing industrial processes. Until such studies are undertaken any firm conclusions would be premature. The findings related in the rest of this paper should therefore be regarded as tentative propositions about group relations within a racially mixed industrial structure.

The following discussion deals only with our information on trade unionism.[15] This constitutes a small part of our total study, but it is of direct relevance to the issues raised in the foregoing sections and covers an empirical area hitherto largely neglected in race-relations research in Britain.[16] The question of membership and participation in unions by coloured immigrants is relevant in two ways. First, the integration of such workers into unions can be seen as a positive step towards fuller incorporation within the industrial and political structure. Questions of their willingness and ability to participate are frequently raised, but rarely investigated. Second, unions have an ideology that accords with non-discrimination on racial grounds, but formal and informal practices are known to exist that militate against official policies. In so far as the trend in negotiations is away from centrally controlled policies towards workshop bargaining, the attitudes and activities of local trade unionists to ethnic minorities become more significant.

Before considering these two dimensions it is necessary to outline the industrial and occupational context within which both unions and coloured immigrant workers are operating. Our perspective was that trade unionism is to be seen as a feature of industrial society, so that in seeking to explain the particular relationships developing between coloured workers and unions it was necessary to investigate them within the industrial totality of Bradford.

THE INDUSTRIAL AND OCCUPATIONAL STRUCTURE
RELATED TO DEGREE OF UNIONIZATION

In overall terms we found, not unexpectedly, that coloured immigrant workers are less unionized than white workers, 16·2 per cent compared to 46·0 per cent. This over-all figure becomes more meaningful when examined in terms of industry groups. An analysis of the industrial variation in membership showed that unionization is not uniformly high for white workers or uniformly low for coloured workers.

TABLE I

Union membership as a percentage of estimated maximum possible membership by industry groups

	Tex-tiles, %	Print-ing, %	Build-ing, %	Engineer-ing, %	Service indus-tries, %	Trans-port, %	Public ser-vices, %	All, %
Coloured workers	10·4	100	65·6	48·4	n.a.	89·9	37·7	16·2
Indigenous labour	44·2	95·6	64·2	68·1	13·3	96·1	76·8	46·0

Note: Maximum possible membership is based on estimates supplied by trade-union officials.

Both groups show a wide range in degree of unionization. The industrial variation, by rank order of industry for the two groups of workers is shown in *Table 2*.

The similarity in terms of rank order indicates the influence of the industrial situation on unionization.[17] Printing and transport have a high degree of unionization, whereas textiles and service industries are relatively low in organization. The largest discrepancy in rank order is found in the public service industry, which for white workers takes precedence over both engineering and building but for coloured immigrant workers ranks lower than both these industries. The probable explanation of this discrepancy

TABLE 2

Rank order of industry	Indigenous labour	Immigrant (coloured) labour
1	Transport	Printing
2	Printing	Transport
3	Public services	Building
4	Engineering	Engineering
5	Building	Public services
6	Textiles	Textiles
7	Service industries	*

* No figure is available for service industries, but our observations reveal no reason to assume that membership would be high relative to other industry groups.

arises from the occupational differences between white and coloured workers. Coloured immigrants in public service tend to be recruited into the lower unskilled levels, whereas the white workers are concentrated in skilled and white-collar positions. The industries in which people work, whatever their ethnic background, are therefore an important factor in the degree of unionization.

Moreover, coloured immigrant workers are also heavily concentrated in industries and occupations in which the unions have been traditionally weak. Particularly, two-thirds of them in Bradford are employed in the textile industry, which is an industry in which unionization among indigenous workers is abnormally low. Textile unions are strongest among craftsmen, e.g. woolsorters, overlookers, and those employed in the dyeing and finishing sections. Few coloured immigrants are found in these occupations. They are concentrated in the combing and spinning sections doing jobs in which unionization has never been strong. An interesting parallel is suggested here with the experience of women in the manufacturing side of the textile industry. The union catering for these sections had a majority of women in the rank and file. Woollen textiles was marked by seasonal fluctuations and irregular bouts of short-time working, and women were regarded as a suitably uncommitted and changeable source of relatively cheap semi-skilled labour. Despite the preponderance of women in the rank and file, full-time women officers have not been a customary feature in Bradford. Women were found in low-level positions such as collectors, and as organizers with a specific field of responsibility. The top positions were held by men. The position of coloured immigrants is similar in many ways, and attitudes arising from this seem to have persisted as coloured immigrants have replaced women. The union encourages the appointment of 'intelligent' English-speaking coloured immigrants as collectors and carefully chooses those considered suitable to act in a liaison and advisory capacity to full-time officials. They do not, however, carry out industrial functions related to negotiating and collective bargaining (see below p. 120 for a comparison with Pakistani views on this development).

In an occupational comparison of union membership further confirmation is found of the lower degrees of unionization being directly related to the position of coloured immigrants in the occupational structure of the city. Analysis of coloured immigrant membership by type of union is shown in *Table 3*.

There are clearly relatively few coloured immigrants in white-collar or craft jobs for unions to recruit, and the number of skilled manual workers is clearly understated since not all skilled workers are recruited by craft unions. 'General and industrial unions' refers to those branches recruiting all grades of worker. The figure for the number of immigrants in white-collar jobs is obviously too low for the city as a whole. White-collar positions open to coloured immigrants, particularly in immigrant-owned businesses, have increased since the survey was carried out. One difficulty we found in collecting accurate statistical data was the reluctance of employers to classify non-manual workers as immigrants.[18] Above a certain occupational level it became inappropriate to recognize employees as coloured immigrants, a category thought to be more readily applicable to the lower grades. However, in terms of membership density, the position of coloured immigrants reflects the over-all situation. Where organization is low, coloured immigrant unionization is lower.

TABLE 3

	General and industrial unions	Craft unions	White-collar unions
Number of replies *	37	14	11
Total membership	18,749	5,568	4,090
Coloured immigrant membership	975	4	2
Coloured immigrants as % of total membership	5·2	0·007	0·005
Potential coloured immigrant membership	6,662	6	2
Potential total membership	58,423	6,142	5,236
Total membership density	32·1	90·7	78·1
Coloured immigrant membership density	14·7	66·7	100

* Questionnaires were sent to 87 union officials, 62 of whom replied.

PARTICIPATION IN UNION ACTIVITY

Coloured immigrants are under-unionized not only in terms of membership but also in terms of active participation in the union. It may be argued that it is early for them to have emerged as union officers. However, some coloured immigrants have been working in Bradford for as long as fifteen years, often in the same industry. Some explanation of the situation may be derived from the attributes of coloured immigrants themselves. On the assumption that English is a necessary qualification for active participation at this level, many would automatically be excluded. Nevertheless, in some sections of industry, transport for instance, there are high concentrations of literate, English-speaking coloured immigrants and it is from among these that potential union officers could be expected to emerge. There are only thirteen part-time coloured immigrant union officials. Two are branch committee members in the transport sector, three are shop stewards, and eight are collectors in the textile industry. There are no coloured immigrant officials in branches in which coloured immigrants are in a minority. It may be inevitable that at this stage coloured immigrant trade-union officers should largely represent coloured immigrant workers within the union. This will be particularly so where language problems exist. It would seem an undesirable development if such a tendency became established so that separate ethnic representation emerged within trade unions. Such a position will presumably be avoided only if the local officials themselves take an active part in promoting multi-ethnic representation. Unions with racially mixed memberships and established education courses would be in the best position to initiate such a policy. There are no coloured immigrants on the local Trades Council, although some of the unions represented on that body have a sizeable immigrant membership.

A general picture thus emerges of the coloured immigrants' contact with the unions being limited, in terms of both membership and participation in union affairs. One reason appears to be that they are concentrated in industrial and occupational sectors where unions have always been weak. This situation applies also to groups of white workers and can be seen as a particular manifestation of the more general problem of organizing and effectively representing certain grades within the industrial structure. The weak unions have tended to pursue a defensive membership policy, concentrating attention on conserving membership where they are strongest, in order to transmit improvements in earnings and conditions of work to the weaker sectors, by using the principle of the maintenance of customary differentials.

The implications of this policy in a multiracial situation are a potential source of racial friction and can be used as bases for racial stereotypes by both immigrants and officials. In such a situation the task of reconciling trade-union policies with the improvement of race relations is a difficult one. An awareness of the nature of the problem can only be a beginning.

UNIONS AND COLOURED IMMIGRANT WORKERS

We also examined the position of the unions in the recruitment and participation of immigrants. The data were collected by interviews with union officials and members of the Trades Council and by postal questionnaires sent to officials of all unions represented in the Bradford area. Interviews were held with officials of those unions catering for the main industries or occupations in which coloured immigrants are employed as well as with those who had publicly expressed views on coloured immigrants, not necessarily in relation to trade unionism. The postal questionnaire was sent to 87 union officials of whom 62 replied.

There is no reason in terms of industrial relations why unions in a relatively weak position should not continue to pursue their traditionally defensive policy when the ethnic composition of the work-groups changes. Many charges of alleged discrimination against union officials can be accounted for in terms of their position in relation to the industrial situation rather than in terms of the ethnic composition of the work-force. However, there have been cases in which formerly weak sections of an industry have become organized by activity of such groups as the Indian Workers Association. Trade-union officials may then be unprepared for dealing with the changed situation, and slowness in responding to requests for assistance may be interpreted as discrimination. In general, what emerges is that, despite a detailed knowledge of occupations within their organizational interest, very few officials related the problems they themselves faced to the question of immigrant membership. They frequently lacked information about the attitudes or behaviour of coloured immigrant workers and were not able to relate their particular problems to the general employment situation in the Bradford area.

The recruitment of coloured immigrants is a function of the knowledge, attitudes, and employment situation of the immigrants and the policy, methods, and attitudes of the unions and their local officials. To the question 'Do you have any specific difficulties in the recruitment of immigrants?' the most frequent response from local officials was that no special difficulties were met with in the recruitment of immigrants. Craft union officials, for instance, said that proof of proficiency in their craft or trade-union membership in their country of origin was sufficient. In transport, an official stated, 'No, most are quite ready to join the trade union when approached.'

The second most frequent response was that the question did not apply because immigrants were not employed in the trades from which the union recruited. A number of reasons given for the non-employment of immigrants are summarized in *Table 4*. Inadequate qualifications and training were reasons given particularly in craft and non-manual unions, but there was one case in which an official of a general union gave this as a reason.

TABLE 4

Reasons for non-employment of immigrants, frequency of mention

Inadequate intelligence	Inadequate qualifications and/or training	Lack of reference	Colour bar by employers	Bad workers	No reason given
1	13	4	3	1	3

Many of this group of respondents explicitly said there was no bar to coloured immigrants being admitted to trade unions, but a few alleged that employers barred them. We have no evidence that unions actively take part in this exclusion process. We do know of cases where unions have been active in preventing adult coloured immigrants who have not served a British apprenticeship from being appointed to supervisory positions.

Where difficulties of recruitment were experienced a number of explanations were advanced. Typical of the views expressed was that of a secretary of a union catering for semi-skilled and unskilled labour: 'Any amount of the above people who are quite eligible for membership do not understand and are afraid to come forward through lack of ability to speak or write English.' He went on to say, 'We do not seem to get the trust and understanding of these people – we are taking them in good faith but suffer the lack of language of Pakistanis and Indians.' A white-collar union official commented that he had asked a few coloured workers to join, but they thought he was trying to victimize them. Coloured immigrants in textiles were thought by one textile union official to be reluctant to join because they worked excessively long hours to please their employers. Many of the statements made by the officials interviewed were conflicting and contradictory. Generally the onus for the low level of union membership was thought to lie with the coloured immigrants themselves. Many comments reflected straightforward stereotyping of racial groups, attributing the qualities of particular workers to their ethnicity and assuming this to be sufficient explanation of their reluctance to join unions. But some officials saw the difficulties in recruiting as due to a lack of interest stemming from particular characteristics assumed to be part of the immigrant's situation. These included his lack of English; the cultural gap, resulting in failure to understand the functions of unions and to emphasis on particular problems of religion and customary habits; the difference in attitude to work, involving a willingness to work long hours; a concern with immediate financial reward, with little weight being given to the conditions under which it was earned. Among those experiencing difficulties there was a widespread view that immigrants are not interested in joining unions, and that those who do join become disillusioned with the ineffectiveness of the union. Only one official mentioned the similarity of their attitudes to those of any newcomers to a particular industry.

With only two exceptions, all the officials felt that their unions were doing everything possible to involve coloured immigrants in union affairs. For those who did not experience any difficulty in recruitment this was a reasonable assumption. For others this attitude was less realistic. In recruiting, a few unions have issued leaflets in Asian languages, particularly Urdu.[19] But the attempts to recruit have remained on the level of formal communication. More active participation was seen as a problem of overcoming particular difficulties with regard to immigrant workers through the appointment of immigrant members to act in a liaison capacity.

It would be inappropriate to attribute the low level of membership and participation to active discrimination by union officials. The situation must be seen within the total industrial context and due allowance made for the general problems of recruitment and involvement that these officials face. However, this evidence indicates that many officials have been unable to define or come to terms with the particular problems of involving immigrants in the union structure.

PAKISTANI EMPLOYEES AND TRADE UNIONISM

The following discussion will deal only with the evidence on Pakistanis.[20] They are regarded in many ways as presenting the most intractable problems for trade-union recruitment and involvement on the grounds of language and cultural differences and the higher incidence of ethnic segregation in the work situation.

The attitudes and behaviour of Pakistanis in relation to trade unionism have not previously been systematically investigated. The interviews were designed to encourage the expression of opinion about unions, as well as to collect information on actual behaviour in terms of membership and knowledge of and contact with unions. The interviews with Pakistanis were conducted mainly in languages other than English.[21]

Union Members

Of 187 Pakistanis, only 27 were, at the time of interviewing, members of trade unions. They had been recruited to unions mainly through friends or workmates (15), 5 claimed to have decided to join on their own initiative. Only 2 were approached to join by trade-union representatives. In terms of knowledge of

English, hours worked, earnings, length of time in England, and job mobility, the members on the whole did not differ from the non-members. These factors are discussed in more detail below.

Language and Length of Stay

All interviewees were asked a general question: 'Do you think trade unions are of any help to immigrants?' Just over half (96) replied that unions were a help, and the remaining 91 thought they were not. Since the language barrier is assumed by union officials to be of some significance both as a problem and as an explanation of the behaviour of Pakistanis, we examined the relationship between language and attitude to unions. In general terms it appears that fluency in English favourably influences attitudes towards unions, but that imperfect knowledge or total lack of English has comparatively little effect. The number of respondents with fluent English who thought trade unions helpful was twice that of those who thought them not helpful. But, conversely, those with no English at all are almost equally divided between the 'helpful' and the 'not helpful' categories.[22] The marginal significance of language in influencing attitudes points to the necessity of looking at the problem in terms of more complex interactions rather than generalizing about the significance of language barriers.

Among those with fluent English only 11 out of 57 were actually union members and, of these, 9 members had been in England for over five years, but so had 23 non-members. Out of 30 who spoke no English, only one was a union member and he had been in England over four years; but 17 of the non-union members had been here for more than five years. The largest group, those with a working knowledge of English, provided 15 members and 85 non-members. The members had all been in England for over two years; four-fifths of them for over four years. The longer experience of England, and the ability to communicate and be communicated with, can be said to predispose towards union membership, but taken alone these factors are insufficient to explain differences in behaviour and attitudes towards unions. It is not correct to imagine that merely mechanical improvements in communication are

E

necessary or that simple exposure to the industrial situation is sufficient to produce a change in outlook or behaviour.

Hours and Earnings

Hours worked and earnings received were put forward as possible obstacles to union membership among immigrants. These factors are frequently cited as explanations for the reluctance of individuals, white or coloured, to join unions. Pakistani workers in Bradford are assumed by many to work long hours from choice – and some of the figures quoted would require superhuman strength and endurance to secure fulfilment. 'They will work eighty hours' or 'They work continuously through two shifts of the three-shift system' were comments frequently recorded during our research. Needless to say, respondents always quoted these hours for firms other than their own. Our evidence from interviews with the Pakistanis showed that by far the largest proportion (111) worked no overtime at all. Several respondents emphasized that they preferred not to work long hours – especially those over forty years of age who were anxious to conserve their health. Fifty worked more than ten hours overtime as a weekly average. These figures do not support the proposition that long hours are responsible for the lack of trade unionists. The relationship between actual union membership among Pakistanis and hours worked is not significant. The trade unionists were divided roughly into two categories: slightly less than half of them (12) worked either no overtime or less than four hours weekly; but the remainder worked over five hours extra, and 6 of them worked in excess of fifteen hours overtime a week. Allowing for the small numbers involved, the tentative conclusion from our evidence is that hours worked cannot properly be cited as a disincentive or incentive to union membership.

Equally, the suggestion that high earnings in any way do act as a deterrent to greater union membership is not borne out by our evidence. Briefly, the average weekly earnings for our respondents was £16.16s.0d. at a time when the national average of weekly earnings for men over twenty-one was £20.12s.0d.[23] The distribution of average net earnings of union members did not differ in any significant way from that of non-members.

Knowledge of Unions

Lack of knowledge about unions at their place of work was common. Out of 152 textile workers, only 60 knew that a union existed and only 12 were aware of the name of the particular union involved. Indirectly, then, the lack of visibility of the unions in the workplace seems to provide a real obstacle to recruitment. Short bursts of recruiting activity are insufficient in a situation where a more continuous and meaningful presence is lacking. The absence of vertical contact on the simple level of organization is a question not only of visibility but of the 'image' that a union projects in particular situations. One of the only two mass strikes in the textile industry for many years followed an agreement between management and unions on a highly complex system of measured production that involved planned redundancies. The workers, predominantly coloured immigrants, were not contacted or consulted until a few days before the introduction of the new scheme. The union was inevitably seen as not only white but as part of the management structure in this case. The labour force reacted by striking, and attempts were made to start a 'coloured people's union'.

In so far as the only contacts with union officials are in such situations the unions become identified with the management and recruitment problems are thus increased.

However, in other industries this has not always been the case. In transport the union was more visible, new recruits were asked to join by their union representatives and supervisory staff as well as fellow-workers, and the procedures of negotiation and consultation were more apparent. The coloured immigrant membership was not only proportionately higher but also more active.

Perception of Unions

The explanations given by the interviewees for their responses to the question whether they thought unions were helpful or not helpful presents us with a clearer picture of the unions as seen by Pakistani workers. The largest category of positive responses (40) looked to the unions to secure better working-conditions, higher wages, and greater representation. That is, they expected unions to fulfil their traditional industrial functions and to bring definite results. Thirty others emphasized their strength and potential helpfulness, but attributed the lack of their apparent success to the absence of cooperation and of interest and forcefulness among the Pakistanis themselves. Among the positive responses there was a marked tendency towards qualified and heavily guarded explanations of their general attitude.

A number of comments made clear that active support was conditional upon the removal of alleged discriminatory practices. For instance, '[they could help] if they want to – but they are under pressure from English workers'; 'if they realized our expectations of them, but they are not anxious to help'; 'they should not exploit immigrant workers'. Some were more specific, 'they control overtime and other conditions and can make the authorities more favourable' and 'theoretically they are good, but they are dominated by those who are underhand'. Some thought they could be helpful, 'if they relax procedure and admit us'. Only two respondents thought Pakistani spokesmen were necessary, but others stressed the need for equality of treatment and for Pakistanis to be active to ensure that unions were helpful.

Among those whose attitude was negative, 31 could give no explanation of their general negative attitude, except to say in many cases that they had no experience of trade-union activity. Contrary to the beliefs held by some union officials that identification with management interests was common among coloured immigrant workers, only 3 Pakistanis gave this as an explanation of their negative attitude to unions. The largest category of negative responses (23) from those who did amplify their general approach did not go beyond expressing despair at getting any help from unions. A further 21 said either 'they stand for English workers' or 'they don't want to include us – they are prejudiced and seek to exploit us'. The remainder gave a variety of explanations; most of which regarded unions as hostile to them and therefore incapable of acting on their behalf. Only one respondent proposed that separate unions should be formed by and for coloured immigrant workers, and this not because of perceived hostility but because he thought that the existing unions 'don't realize our problems'.

In all the responses, both positive and negative, there is obvious concern at the perceived level of discriminatory practices and pre-judiced attitudes. How far this can explain the low level of member-ship is not clear. It certainly does not influence the general approach to unions in one (negative) direction only. But it may be sufficient, even where there is a positive approach, to hinder recruitment if other conditions in the workplace, including the level and type of union activity, do not expressly encourage membership.

Cultural v. *Instrumental Attitudes*

Finally, we consider more fully the perceptions that Pakistanis have of the role of unions and how far this role was fulfilled in relation to immigrant workers. The Pakistanis are frequently cited as the group with the greatest degree of cultural difference from the indigenous work-force, greater than that among other coloured immigrants, notably Indians and West Indians. How far such cultural differences create obstacles to the processes of their in-corporation within the industrial situation is still an open question in terms of the available evidence. It is by no means clear, for instance, how far Pakistani work groups are intentionally self-segregating or are products of the demands of particular industrial situations or policies.[24] Nevertheless, cultural differences are seen as 'problems' in that difficulties in recruiting and retaining union members are attributed to them by union officials. These difficulties are thought to arise both from concern with different issues and from a lack of understanding of the role and functions of unions. The view that emerges from an analysis of the respondents' stated expectations is, however, rather different. The replies were classi-fied as 'cultural', 'industrial', and 'cultural/industrial'. Of the 98 respondents who thought unions could be helpful, 12 referred to cultural issues only, 76 to industrial issues, and 10 to a combination of cultural and industrial. Twenty-two respondents, therefore, gave some weight to cultural factors such as religious holidays and breaks for prayers. But the needs of Pakistanis as industrial workers were clearly given more emphasis. Their concern was with wages,

E2

hours, and conditions of work rather than with special consideration on cultural grounds. The majority called for direct representation in the structure of the union, especially where they were a
majority on the shop floor. These were not demands for liaison
officers but for officials with customary trade-union functions
elected by Pakistanis. This demand for Pakistani representatives
was because they believed their industrial demands would be more
effectively pursued by Pakistanis than by white representatives
whom they thought were hostile. The use of liaison officers, which
is regarded by some union officials as a solution, does not seem
to meet the demands of Pakistanis who consider that unions have
something to offer them as industrial workers.

The above discussion illustrates the interrelationship of industrial structure and the attitudes and behaviour of groups within it.
In the opposing explanations put forward by union officials and
Pakistanis for the low level of union activity among Pakistanis, both
parties show a lack of awareness of the general problem of involvement within particular industrial situations and ignore many of the
situational variations. They perceive the difficulties largely in terms
of the attitudes and activities or attributes of the other group. This
common-sense and obvious interpretation is then part of the
definition of the situation and becomes a disintegrative process
among employees and their representatives. On the one hand,
there are union officials who see their organizations as open to all
workers, but emphasize cultural and racial differences as problems.
On the other, there are Pakistanis who stress to an unexpected
degree their role as employees and the need for effective representation, but perceive the unions as hostile and ineffective and attribute this to racial attitudes on the part of whites.

One result of the inability of the unions to act on behalf of
Pakistanis on the shop-floor has been the development of informal
groups of workers acting collectively. In one case, typical of a
number of incidents over the past few years, a group of Pakistani
workers were involved in a dispute with management over bonus
payments. A Pakistani spokesman expressed the grievances of the
group and was dismissed by the management. As a result, the
group of 25 men walked out of the shift. Of this group only 2 were

paid-up members of the union, although 15 had been members at various times. All expressed the view that the officials had not assisted them, and they had ceased to pay dues. They had then appointed one of their number, who spoke English, to act as their representative in any negotiations with the management of their firm. In response to a hostile act by management, this group acted collectively using accepted trade-union methods, but outside the formal union framework.

Such informally organized action makes the position of the unions even more difficult, since they are bound by agreements that preclude their acting on behalf of unofficial strikers. This in turn serves to support the belief that they are unwilling to assist Pakistanis.

CONCLUSIONS

The substantive findings in this paper, though concerned largely with a specific industrial structure, point to general problem areas within the field of inter-ethnic industrial relations. Systematic evidence on multiracial collective action and organization in Britain is lacking at the present time.[25] Our evidence indicating many of the obstacles to such organization needs to be treated with caution until the conditions underlying multiracial industrial activity have been more closely investigated.

It is still problematic how far the failure to involve coloured workers in union activity will encourage them to form separate organizations in attempts to obtain effective representation. Informal collective action along these lines has not yet been transformed into permanent organizations. How far it will be depends not only on union policies and practices but also on the extent to which jobs are more clearly allocated in colour terms, thus providing a basis for such organization. Strongly organized unions are in a position to represent their members in an effective way. Where they are also able to control entry to particular trades or shops they can discriminate against particular categories of workers. In this situation there is combined the possibility of positive action and policies to incorporate or to exclude coloured workers. It is these

unions which will be increasingly relevant to the employment opportunities of coloured employees brought up and educated in
Britain. Unions unable to pursue effective policies in representing
the interests of their members are vulnerable to charges of discrimination from coloured workers. Since they are also likely to be in
those industries and occupations in which immigrant workers find
employment most easily their problems of organization are crucial
to multiracial developments. If those within such situations faced
with common predicaments attribute the failure to deal with shared
problems to racial characteristics or discrimination, as our evidence
indicates, then the unions may be further weakened by withdrawal
into non-unionism by sections of their potential membership. And
economic and social issues are more likely to be transformed into
racial conflicts. There is little indication, however, of any general
awareness of these dangers among local officials of unions.

Notes

1 See Milton M. Gordon (1961) for a critical discussion of these processes.
2 H. M. Blalock (1967: 199–203) comments on the problems involved
   in investigations of race and class prejudice and indicates the necessity for an awareness of class and race as separate phenomena. John
   C. Leggett (1968) attempts to relate these systematically in his study
   carried out in the United States. There is no comparable study of
   the British situation of the kind undertaken by Leggett.
3 The term immigrant has come in popular usage to refer mainly to
   coloureds, whether immigrant or not. It is therefore difficult to use
   without invalid connotations. In this study immigrant is used to
   apply strictly to those who have migrated to Britain. Wherever
   possible the various groups are designated as Pakistanis, Indians,
   etc. The collective term coloured immigrant, though clumsy, is
   necessary. In our survey we constantly faced problems of terminology, and accuracy was at times sacrificed to the use of terms most
   readily understood.
4 Eric Butterworth (1967: 3, *Table 1*) estimated that the population of
   Bradford included 15,000 Pakistanis, 4,000 Indians, and 2,000 West
   Indians. Estimates of the working population are less easily arrived
   at. On the basis of our returns, the total of employed Indians, West

Indians, and Pakistanis amounted to 7,500. This is probably a minimal figure. There is evidence of members of these groups living in Bradford but working outside.

5 Others were already working in this field and there are now several published works, notably Hepple (1968), Wright (1968), Patterson (1968).

6 This was claimed to be the case not only in the field of employment but also in housing and more particularly in education.

7 Our research began before the publication of the PEP Report on Racial Discrimination and the first of the Powell speeches on immigration.

8 This was in reply to a request for basic information on numbers and types of jobs relating to coloured immigrants in one large undertaking. Some of the very real problems of coloured immigrants employed by this undertaking were constantly and openly discussed at meetings in the city.

9 This problem is of even greater importance at the present time and the difficulty of selecting and training 'acceptable' interviewers appears to have been given very little consideration in Britain. The use of social workers or undergraduate students to investigate immigrant problems is unlikely to produce useful information.

10 Subsequently a small case study was carried out mainly in one section of the wool industry in a West Riding town, see B. C. Cohen and P. J. Jenner (1968).

11 It is interesting but not unexpected to note that reports that have reached Pakistan of hostility towards and poor conditions of Pakistanis in Britain are in some cases interpreted in terms of the low status of those who have migrated. The implications of this for relations between the Pakistani immigrants and their government representatives here is as yet unexplored.

12 See Blalock (1967) for a discussion of proposed investigations of this type.

13 For instance, despite the sociological literature on American trade unions there has been very little attention given to the development of labour organizations in terms of relations with Negro workers. A recent study (Jacobson ed. 1968) leads to a questioning of many of the assumptions involved in earlier work.

14 John Archer Jackson's (1963) study of the Irish has some interesting insights into the situation of Irish immigrants in employment.

15 The research was conducted over a three-year period, 1966–9. Employers, trade-union officials, and coloured immigrant workers were interviewed. Material was collected on the work situation of

    coloured immigrants from the first stages of securing employment, through experiences at work, including pay and conditions and promotion, to job mobility.

16 See in this context Hepple (1968: 82–6) for a brief survey of trade-union practices in relation to immigrant and coloured workers, and Radin (1966) for expressed attitudes of officials.

17 A similar influence is found when the degree of unionization among women is analysed by industry groups.

18 More than once returns were made showing a number of coloured immigrant workers in manual grades but omitting those in non-manual grades. In some cases our evidence from other sources showed that coloured immigrants were employed, though in small numbers, in non-manual positions.

19 One union official claimed a 33 per cent increase in membership in 1966, most of which was made up of coloured immigrant workers. The East Pakistanis speak Bengali and many of the West Pakistanis use Punjabi. There are also several hundred Kashmiris, few of whom read Urdu.

20 Our sample was drawn up in terms of the number of coloured immigrants estimated to be working in Bradford industries. (Questionnaires were sent to 550 employers, which covered 90 per cent of the working population of Bradford. The response rate in terms of number of employees amounted to 75 per cent. The number of firms employing coloured immigrants was 223, which between them had a total of 66,845 in all grades.) The sample is therefore representative in terms of industrial distribution rather than of ethnicity of the workers. In our sample of 224 Pakistanis, 25 were self-employed and therefore not relevant to trade unionism, and 12 interviews were not complete on this point, leaving a total of 187 Pakistanis.

21 The problem of interviewer bias was recognized as inevitable, particularly since literacy in English and another language frequently implies a status differential. However, an attempt was made to avoid using interviewers known to have official connections, e.g. Pakistani High Commission representatives, social workers, liaison officers, or local businessmen. These are the people most usually used and quoted. Our interviewers were selected to avoid the disadvantages usually incorporated, perhaps unknowingly, by those less well acquainted with the Pakistani population of Bradford and its intricate social structure. Our interviewers were teachers, postgraduate students, and clerks mainly living and working outside Bradford. The interviewers were matched to the respondents in terms of ethnicity and language.

22 Three language categories for respondents were used. None, Working Knowledge, and Fluent English.

Knowledge of English	Trade unions Helpful	Not helpful
None	14	16
Working knowledge	43	57
Fluent	39	18
	96	91

23 *Ministry of Labour Gazette*, January 1968, pp. 82–3.
24 The evidence from our survey of employment suggests that policies pursued by managements within a particular labour-demand situation are particularly influential in this respect. For instance, in textiles almost all night shifts in the combing sections are staffed by Pakistanis. The manager of a manmade-fibre top-making firm commented, 'I couldn't think of starting a night-shift without thirty or forty Pakistanis.'
25 The Barbican strike during 1966–7, in which more than half the strikers were coloured, and the strikes at Fords during 1969 are such examples; but equally the Courtauld's dispute in 1965 provides contrary evidence. Investigations, not only of strikes, but also of multiracial union activity at all levels, are still awaited.

ACKNOWLEDGEMENTS

I should like to thank Harold Wolpe, who read and commented on an earlier draft of this paper. My thanks are due to the Survey of Race Relations for financial assistance towards the costs of interviewing and for permission to use material already included in my two reports submitted to them on 'The Employment Situation of Immigrants from India, Pakistan, and the West Indies working in the Bradford Area'.

References

BLALOCK, H. M. 1967. *Toward a Theory of Minority-Group Relations.* New York: Wiley.
BUTTERWORTH, ERIC (ed.) 1967. *Immigrants in West Yorkshire.* Institute of Race Relations.

COHEN, B. C., & JENNER, P. J. 1968. The Employment of Immigrants: A Case Study within the Wool Industry. *Race* 10 (1).

GORDON, MILTON M. 1961. Assimilation in America: Theory and Reality. *Daedalus* 90.

HEPPLE, BOB 1968. *Race, Jobs and Law in Britain*. London: Allen Lane, The Penguin Press.

JACKSON, JOHN ARCHER 1963. *The Irish in Brtiain*. London: Routledge and Kegan Paul.

JACOBSON, JULIUS (ed.) 1968. *The Negro and the American Labour Movement*. New York: Anchor Books, Doubleday.

LEGGETT, JOHN C. 1968. *Class, Race and Labor*. New York: Oxford University Press.

PATTERSON, SHEILA 1968. *Immigrants in Industry*. London: Oxford University Press.

RADIN, B. 1966. Coloured Workers and British Trade Unions. *Race* 8 (2).

WRIGHT, PETER 1968. *The Coloured Worker in British Industry*. London: Oxford University Press.

NICHOLAS DEAKIN

Race, the Politicians, and Public Opinion
A Case Study

Myths flourish with special hardiness in the field of race relations; all assumptions made about it need to be scrutinized with particular care. One that has produced a particularly luxuriant crop of subsidiary beliefs concerns the state of public opinion on what is characterized as the 'immigrant problem' and the role that it should play in the formation of policy. Certain specific beliefs under this general head are examined in this paper. They are, first of all, the view that the propensity to reject immigrants varies in intensity between different areas. That is, that rejection increases as a result of local circumstances – the number of immigrants present or existing social conditions upon which they are assumed to impose additional strain – or general variations in the local social, historical, and political background. A second set of linked assumptions concerns leaders of local opinion in the areas concerned. These involve the extent to which such leaders share the views of their constituents and how they perceive their function in relation to the 'immigrant problem'. For from the assumption that widespread hostility exists, there has developed a theory of leadership (whose most notable exponent is Mr Enoch Powell) that holds that it is the duty of politicians to provide a 'safety valve' in a situation of tension. This view clearly depends for its legitimacy not only on a distinctive view of the representative function of elected members of local and national bodies, but also on the accuracy of the perception of hostility. Data from two recent investigations provide an opportunity to test these assumptions against empirical evidence. The first is a small-scale study of opinion leaders conducted by the present writer and some colleagues immediately after the general election of 1966.[1] The second is the large-scale survey of attitudes towards coloured minorities in areas of substantial immigrant settlement conducted for the Survey of Race Relations in the winter of 1966–7 (Abrams 1969). Both investigations cover the same Black Country borough – Wolverhampton. Taken together, the results provide a composite picture of the state of opinions at various levels in the community and, to some extent, of their interaction.

THE LEVEL OF HOSTILITY

The first important finding from the large-scale survey of attitudes is that the stereotype of the borough as an area that has had considerable experience of immigration and displays an unusually high level of hostility towards the newcomers has some validity.

The preliminary analysis of the 524 interviews completed in the borough shows that, of all the boroughs studied, Wolverhampton respondents claimed the highest rate of contact with immigrants. Sixty-three per cent said that they lived near (five minutes' walk or closer) to immigrants and 9 per cent claimed to have them as neighbours. Half had been in this situation for more than three years. Of all parents, 77 per cent claimed that their children went to school with coloured pupils and, of workers, 49 per cent claimed to have worked alongside coloured workers. Seventy-nine per cent had ridden on a bus with a coloured conductor (this is hardly surprising, considering the recruitment policy of the municipal transport authority). Informal contact in bus queues was also reported on a substantial scale. In all these situations of contact, with the partial exception of the workplace, Wolverhampton residents reported more difficulties than respondents from other boroughs; their rejection of outsiders was particularly strong in the case of Indians. Hostility was also particularly noticeable in the field of education; the preliminary analysis comments that 'there were more cases of difficulty with all 3 nationalities (from Wolverhampton) than for any other town' although such difficulties were reported in only 19 per cent of all cases. Similarly, unfortunate experiences with bus conductors and poor relationships in the neighbourhood were reported more frequently than in the case of other areas. Only in employment did contact with coloured workers tend to modify attitudes in a favourable direction.

When asked whether coloured workers should be dismissed before white ones on grounds of colour alone, Wolverhampton respondents with experience of coloured workmates were significantly less inclined to agree to such dismissals than were those with no such experience.

Generally, although the level of outright rejection is not high, it remains significantly higher for Wolverhampton than for other boroughs. Another significant deviation is that Labour supporters in the borough are more inclined to adopt hostile attitudes than in other areas and that in this neighbourhood working-class hostility is more strongly marked.

What such findings do not explain is the extent to which there is a causal connection between the experience of contact in the local context and the expression of hostility – in other words, whether the simple explanation of the rejection of outsiders by reference to local conditions or their numbers will hold water.

THE LOCAL CONTEXT

The West Midland conurbation as a whole is, as the Regional Study of 1965 puts it:

'. . . a pepperpot mixture of nineteenth and twentieth century, with renewal and dereliction and industrial and residential areas often cheek by jowl. Some parts are pleasant, especially on the fringes. But there are also widespread areas of mean streets, twilight housing and plain slums. The atmosphere is one of activity, prosperity and growth, but a good deal of congestion and decay as well. The physical scene, in spite of very considerable current efforts at improvement, is still largely dominated by the unlovely heritage of an industrial revolution based on coal, iron, steam, canals and railways – the more so perhaps because the economy here, as in many of the towns near by, still rests primarily on the production and working of metals. This combination of growth and congestion, in an area which although highly prosperous is still much in need of physical renewal, is the conurbation's main problem – and the region's too' (West Midlands Regional Study 1965).

However, Wolverhampton, on the western fringe of the conurbation, has escaped many of the worst consequences of the uninhibited growth of industry in the Black Country. The Moser and Scott indices of social-class composition and housing stress reveal the borough safely in the middle of the league table: an observant journalist comments:

'Of almost anywhere else in the Black Country one might have expected a speech like Enoch Powell's and conceded that at least it was based on some kind of experience: people getting on each other's nerves in the middle of wastelands, broken buildings and vistas of smoke, filthy brick and rosebay willow-herb. But Wolverhampton isn't like that.

A man with his origins in South Lancashire can drive around the town for an afternoon without seeing anything he would pass as a slum until he comes to Bilston, which only became part of Wolverhampton through some local government grafting a couple of years ago. The worst in Wolverhampton proper – Powell's Wolverhampton, and Renée Short's – seems to be some mildly dismal terrace housing (brickwork still glowing with a faint but healthy pink) and some commonplace council semi-detached work that a lot of people in East London would leap at. A man well rooted there reckons that one-third of the borough is industry and the rest residential, a half of that high-class residential, too. He'll be right' (Moorhouse 1968).

At the same time the situation of the inhabitants of the borough displays many of the characteristics described in the composite picture of the conurbation in the Regional Study:

'. . . low national assistance payments but also relatively few personal incomes beyond £1500. Higher than average household expenditure on most things and particularly cars and food, but lower than average spending on services; lower than average rates of drunkenness, indictable offences, suicides and children in care; lower than average proportions of children staying on at school or gaining university awards – bigger than average lists per family doctor and dentist – and less than average spent on prescriptions' (West Midlands Regional Study 1965).

There is, it might be suggested, a certain incongruence between the material prosperity of individuals and the depressed physical environment in which some of them still have to live. This might tend to lead them to lay particular stress on factors that differentiate them from less successful neighbours. To those jealous of such distinctions the arrival of coloured immigrants, attracted by employment opportunities, might be seen as a threat not to material sources but to their status.

But this is speculation. What is solid fact is that Wolverhampton does not have, in terms of the population recorded at the Census, an abnormally large population of immigrants. The enlarged population produced by the local government reorganization of 1966 included, at the sample Census of 1966, 12,700 people born in the three major countries of migration – the West Indies, India, and Pakistan. These formed 4·8 per cent of the total population: nine other local authorities have higher proportions of immigrants – some substantially greater.

These immigrants had been attracted to the borough over the course of the previous dozen years, largely through the opportunities for employment presented by local industry – in particular the foundries and a large tyre factory. They have over that period found little trouble in obtaining and retaining employment; but considerable difficulty has been experienced in the field of housing. This has been frequently described by local politicians, local-authority officials, and those interviewed during the course of the current investigations, as the 'flashpoint'. The local authority owns a substantial proportion of the housing stock in the new borough, and there have been suggestions of discrimination in the letting of accommodation to immigrants. To the extent that a distinction is drawn between native and immigrant applicants in the terms on which their names are placed on the housing list – immigrants have to complete a further year in order to qualify – these allegations have substance. It has been – rather cynically – suggested that the poorer conditions in which they live will act as some form of compensation by providing them with a larger number of points and thereby accelerating qualification. Alternatively, the Chairman of the Housing Committee has referred to the larger size of families, which would have the same effect. But these rationalizations, however relevant in practice, do not explain away the basic policy position adopted by the local authority, nor has the council been able to answer those critics who maintain, as the author of one thorough investigation has done, that there is additional *de facto* discrimination both in the processes of slum clearance and re-housing from clearance schemes and in the allocation of council housing to those who qualify – either through clearance or on the list.

The local authority operates a dispersal policy intended to avoid the growth of 'ghettos'. A coloured family being rehoused is placed at least five houses away from its nearest coloured neighbour. In the case of a block of flats, there would never be more than one coloured family per floor and preferably one to every two floors. However, the council's rehousing policy cuts across the intention to disperse in that immigrants have tended to be allocated to pre-war accommodation. Nearly two-thirds of those rehoused in council accommodation at the time of the present study were rehoused on pre-war estates compared with exactly one-third of all council tenants.[2] Moreover, the majority of 'non-natives' were to be found on a single estate. As one of those involved in the present study has put it:

'This Estate, situated about two miles north-east of the town centre, was built in the inter-war period, and is notable for its lack of social facilities. As one walks around the area, one senses an atmosphere of hopelessness and decadence; broken windows patched with cardboard are not uncommon; light shades are often absent; gardens frequently neglected and strewn with refuse; streets are littered (with both paper and children); garden gates are often missing. The Estate has a reputation for poor standards, and residents are classed as inferior by the average man-in-the-street in Wolverhampton. This, quite naturally, leads many of the residents to apply for transfers to other more reputable estates, which means that the "better" white families move away, leaving behind the "poorer" white element (who are barred by the assessment described above) plus the immigrant community. Hence, relatively large numbers of houses on the Estate become vacant each year. These are filled by families from the waiting list. The process is a continuous one, producing a relatively unstable community.'

By contrast, black faces are rare on post-war estates despite the fact that coloured tenants are as anxious to transfer from the unstable surroundings of the pre-war estate as are the more ambitious natives.

The local authority have said, and there is justice in their claim, that the majority of immigrants are not at this stage interested in council accommodation. However the difficulties experienced by immigrants attempting to obtain property on suburban private housing estates around the city have in practice seriously restricted in location and quality the accommodation available to the immigrants. At the time of this study it was estimated that 1,000 houses owned by immigrants (chiefly Indians) were in multi-occupation. These were largely in the 'better quality but less plentiful and price-inflated, older terraced houses' (Burney 1968) located a mile to a mile and a half from the city centre. Attempts by ambitious immigrants to move further from the centre into better surroundings have in the past been met by active opposition on the part of local white inhabitants. For example, on one relatively new housing estate of some 250 units, a house came up for sale and was to be sold to a coloured family. In order to prevent this, each householder gave £10 to the local residents' association, which then bought the house, reselling it to a white family, and repaying the contributors. A slight loss was made on the transaction, but everyone appeared to think that the result was worth the small loss incurred.[3] These practices have been underpinned by a tacit conspiracy on the part of estate agents and, perhaps most important of all, by the acquiescence of the local authority. Although one area with substantial immigrant settlement has recently been the subject of a clearance scheme, the local authority's role has in practice been mainly confined to ensuring that overcrowding does not become too blatant in immigrant-owned property. The opportunity to encourage the strong drive towards house-ownership by making available mortgage funds has not been taken. And one of the main consequences of the unchecked tendency towards concentration that has resulted has been that a number of schools in the area have begun to receive high percentages of immigrant pupils. These concentrations in certain schools have provided the other 'flashpoint' referred to by respondents during the course of these studies.

However, it must be stressed that despite these high percentages in individual schools the numbers of immigrant children – in the Department of Education and Science definition – in local schools is not exceptionally high: 11·8 per cent of the school population were so categorized in 1968, which places Wolverhampton fifteenth in order among local education authorities in England and Wales.

In short, an explanation of disproportionate resentment derived solely from number and local circumstances will not do. Although certain aspects of the Wolverhampton situation lend themselves to dramatization, explanations of the way in which the area has come to symbolize racial tension must be sought elsewhere. Such explanations, we felt at the outset of the opinion leader study, might be derived from an examination of the political background. These might explain why public opinion had been so slow to make itself felt and why it assumed the forms that it eventually did. A key element in any explanation, it seemed to us, would be the perception by councillors of the state of opinion, the response that it evoked from them, their conception of their role in this situation, and indeed their own opinions.

POLITICAL BACKGROUND

Wolverhampton has, since 1950, had one Member of Parliament from each main political party. Both seats can be described as comparatively safe ones, barring landslides. On the Borough Council control has up to the recent past been in the hands of the Labour Party, although on one famous occasion it depended on the casting vote of the mayor. Thus Wolverhampton is not in any sense a one-party town: political conflict exists and there are tangible rewards to be harvested in successful campaigns. Yet neither at the general election of 1964 nor in 1966 was there any evidence of the issue of coloured immigration breaking the surface. In common with other Black Country seats, the two Wolverhampton constituencies showed lower than average swings towards Labour at the 1964 election and a higher than average swing at that of 1966. But Wolverhampton itself showed no significant variations from the general pattern. Nor did the issue come into the open in local politics during this period.

Indeed, a recent thorough examination of the situation (Jones 1969) shows that although resentment was seen to exist, the topic was not discussed at all in council or in the main local political organizations, up to the point when the local-government reorganization took place. It is true that an independent candidate with openly hostile views towards immigrants won a seat on the council at the election of 1965; but he lost it in the following year.

Yet the fact that there was no formal discussion of the issue does not necessarily imply that no concern was felt. The study of opinion leaders provides an opportunity to judge the extent to which resentment was recognized in 1966, how local leaders assessed its significance, and what action they felt might legitimately flow from their assessment.

OPINION LEADERS AND PERCEPTIONS OF THE SITUATION

In the opinion leaders study, the original intention was to conduct 40 interviews with members of the local authority (that is, half the

total membership, the names being selected at random) and 40
with other local figures – professional men (doctors, clergy), the
local editor, employers, representatives of voluntary organizations,
and trades unionists.

In the event 27 interviews (representing 67 per cent of those
approached) were completed in the first category and 21 (52 per
cent) in the second category. Since the non-members were selected
arbitrarily there is in any case no question of considering the
sample representative, but the low response rate in this category
means that the responses of non-members must be treated with
especial reserve. In addition, an attempt was made to secure additional interviews, 20 in all (10 in each category), in a neighbouring
borough, for comparative purposes. Seventeen interviews were
completed, 7 with members and 10 with non-members. In the
event, distinctions between attitudes of respondents in the two
boroughs appeared to be insignificant and in some cases the responses have been aggregated with the Wolverhampton respondents to form a group of 65 in all.

Initially, an attempt was made to establish the extent of local
loyalties against the background of the enlargement of the borough
(which also affected the neighbouring one). Asked to select a
principal loyalty, half the respondents, taken as a whole, selected
the local borough, 11 per cent the Black Country, 14 per cent the
Midlands, and the remainder some larger unit. As one might
expect, a tendency to select the borough was stronger among
the local-born in the sample than it was among those born elsewhere. But local loyalties did not prevent respondents from expressing criticism about the area.

Fifty-two of the 65 informants felt that the Midlands had
characteristics that differentiated the area from the rest of the
country. In a few cases these were felt to be only good characteristics or only poor characteristics, but the majority felt that the
Midlands had some characteristics that were to be admired, and
others that were to be criticized.

The qualities that were most admired in Midlanders were
friendliness and loyalty, bluntness and frankness, and deter-
mination:

	No. of mentions
Loyalty, or Friendliness	17
Hospitality	2
Community spirit	2
Bluntness, Frankness	8
Practicality, Efficiency	3
Determination	3
Independence	3

Other favourable comments referred to shrewdness, honesty, ruggedness, and the 'cosmopolitan' nature of the area. Criticisms centred upon materialism (which was, however, said to be a national failing by many) isolation and insularity, and resistance to change:

Materialism	7
Greed, Selfishness	3
Isolation, Insularity	5
Resistance to change	4
Resistance to culture	2

Most of those who felt that the Midlands had a character of its own felt that the area could learn from other parts of the country. The comments reflect the criticisms made above; the Midlanders could learn to think more of other people and less of themselves, they could learn to be more tolerant and adaptable and less dogmatic. Other qualities mentioned as being lacking in the area were culture, sophistication, civic pride, thriftiness, and good manners. Respondents were also sceptical about the extent to which a community identity existed. Asked how far people in the area are prepared to join in community activities, whether the area was generally friendly and neighbourly, and whether it was desirable as a part of the country in which to live, Wolverhampton respondents tended to be sceptical. Moreover, in describing the area as 'neighbourly' or 'desirable', respondents referred to material factors like ease of access and ample employment opportunities:

Wolverhampton

	Politicians	Non-politicians
People join in communal activities	14 (52%)	9 (43%)
Area is friendly and neighbourly	22 (82%)	13 (62%)
Desirable area to live in	19 (70%)	12 (57%)

In the main study an attempt was also made to establish the degree of community feeling that exists in areas of immigrant settlement: it was found that Wolverhampton respondents showed a significantly lower rate of community sense measured by the degree of shared interests than did other respondents. The preliminary analysis comments:

'People have little in common but are still committed to others in the neighbourhood, perhaps an extended family. Wolverhampton appears to be a traditional society in the process of disintegration. Commitments remained but the lives and interest of people have begun to diverge.'

Asked about changes in the neighbourhood, 60 per cent of Wolverhampton respondents perceived a change, as opposed to 34 per cent who did not. However, one-third of those who saw change thought it was for the better. This should be set against the pronouncement of one of the town's Members of Parliament that, over twelve years, up to 1966:

'. . . entire areas were transformed by the substitution of a wholly or predominantly coloured population for the previous native inhabitants, as completely as other areas were transformed by the bulldozer' (Powell 1967).

In the sample survey only one-third of those who saw the area as changing for the worse spontaneously referred to coloured people as a cause or index of the area's decline.

PERCEPTIONS OF LOCAL PROBLEMS

All respondents in the opinion leaders survey were asked to identify major local problems. The most widely mentioned local problem was housing, included as a major local problem by two in three informants. Other local issues related to the problems of immigration and overcrowding. The frequency with which they were mentioned by respondents was:

	%
Housing	68
Immigration	46
Road, traffic	18
Education	14
Lack of amenities	8
Overindustrialization	6
Public transport	6
Unemployment	5
Shortage of land	5
Overpopulation	5
Health	3
Town planning	3

There is no evidence that the problems in the two towns were thought to differ, nor do the politically involved informants differ in their views from the non-politicians.

In their comments upon these problems, informants were clearly not unaware of links between them. On closer examination, opinions clustered round two basic problems: general overcrowding and the influence of immigrants. These two problems were seen as generating others: the inadequacy of amenities and facilities, in terms of housing, transport, education, and public health.

Yet despite the perception of immigration as a problem, detailed questioning of the opinion leaders revealed a high degree of complacency about the way in which immigrants were received in the area. Only one of the 65 informants, a Wolverhampton politician, denied the existence of a problem to the extent of failing to identify the existence of minority groups. Respondents felt that the local response had generally been fair.

All Informants (65)

People from other parts of the country are treated:	%
Fairly	84
Unfairly	5
Don't know, not answered	11
Foreigners are treated:	
Fairly	80
Unfairly	13
Don't know, not answered	7
Coloured people are treated:	
Fairly	66
Unfairly	31
Don't know, not answered	3

SOURCES OF DISCRIMINATION

The groups among the local population that were most widely felt by respondents to discriminate against coloured immigrants were the 'less educated', the 'less intelligent', and 'lower-status' workers. Typical statements were:

'The working class are inclined to be the most prejudiced.'
'The lower strata of intelligence [treat coloured people unfairly] not the working classes.'
'The ignorant and less educated people treat coloured people unfairly.'
'Manual workers tend to be more anti-immigrant especially older people.'[4]

A minority of informants also criticized shopkeepers, estate agents, and property-owners.

'Some white people are making unfair profits on property.'
'Some white men sell them condemned property.'

'Estate agents: coloured people have great difficulty getting a house.'
'Some exploitation by salesmen.'

Criticism was not restricted to the local population. A few informants also mentioned discrimination between immigrant groups: Irish versus coloured, Indian versus West Indian. The question of exploitation by coloured landlords was also mentioned.

'At one time there was some friction between coloured people and Irishmen working on a building site – the fault of the Irish.'
'The greatest exploitation is by other coloured people, for example Indian landlords.'
'Foreigners, like Poles and Ukrainians treat coloured people unfairly.'
'Some of the white immigrants (Poles, Hungarians, etc.) tend to treat them [coloured people] rather badly.'

Although coloured groups were most widely mentioned when immigrant groups were mentioned, the existence of European, especially Central European, minorities was also recognized. (It reflects substantial migration by those groups into the area immediately after the Second World War.) The frequency with which various nationalities were mentioned is shown on the next page.

The West Indians were most frequently considered to be making a contribution to the community, through their operation of public services and the performance of functions unattractive to the local population. In a similar way, Indians were also thought to be making a contribution but were credited by some respondents with greater intelligence, leading to a contribution of a more substantial order (though the exact nature of this contribution was not specified).

Indians and Pakistanis were most frequently criticized for a failure to contribute to the community. The criticisms were mainly framed in terms of their inability or unwillingness to assimilate or to be assimilated in terms of language, religion, and social behaviour. It was felt that a group with such major cultural differences (also mentioned, although to a lesser extent, in the case of European immigrants) tended to withdraw and hence play no part in community activities.

	% of respondents mentioning
West Indians, Jamaicans	54
Indians, Sikhs	47
Pakistanis	45
Chinese	7
Poles	35
Ukrainians	8
Hungarians	7
Other Central Europeans	7
Italians	15
Cypriots	2
Other Europeans	6
Irish	18
Welsh	8
Scots	2

'The Indians are more of a separate cultural unit.'

'Indians [contribute least to the community] – I don't know what to make of them. They seem to take more out, although they are intelligent and will contribute later on intellectually.'

'Pakistanis and Indians won't mix, lock themselves away.'

'Pakistanis deny women a place – they differ in religion and culture.'

'The smaller groups like Egyptians and Hungarians who congregate together [contribute least].'

Opinions were divided as to whether, on the whole, foreigners and immigrants contributed more to the community than they took out. This division of opinion was common to politicians and non-politicians:

	All informants (65) %	Politicians (34) %	Non-politicians (31) %
Immigrants			
Contribute	57	55	60
Take out	35	36	34
Don't know	8	9	6

In this respect the opinion leaders differed significantly from the larger sample. This group were asked a broadly similar question: 17 per cent thought that immigrants were no different from others, but 77 per cent of Wolverhampton respondents (compared with 62 per cent overall) thought that West Indians took out more than they contributed and 76 per cent (60 per cent in the aggregated five towns) held the same view of Indians. There were also significant differences between respondents categorized as 'working class' (86 per cent of whom thought that at least one immigrant group took out more than they contributed) and those categorized as 'middle class' (74 per cent of whom held this view). This difference was most marked in Wolverhampton than in any other borough, as was the negative stereotype generally.

Asked to identify the grounds on which the entry of coloured people might be regarded as undesirable, Wolverhampton respondents varied significantly from the national norm in the anxieties they selected. Concern expressed about housing was far below that in the total five-town sample; asked about the allocation of local-authority housing to newcomers, Wolverhampton respondents displayed no marked anxiety. Similarly, the majority would not resist the letting of private accommodation to newcomers. Nor was concern about employment a major factor. However, substantially greater concern was displayed on the question of the hygiene and disease rate of immigrants and slightly greater concern over education and the social services.

The question of the scope and form of remedial action then arises. Since the opinion leaders agreed in defining the goal of policy as integration, the problem can be summed up in a single question: who is responsible for ensuring that integration takes place?

THE LIMITS OF ACTION

Politicians and non-politicians in the opinion leader sample are in agreement; while about half believe that immigrants have an obligation to take the initiative in integrating into the community, the vast majority felt that local people have a duty to help in the process, individually and collectively, and should tolerate the expression of minority views and behaviour.

As in most groups, a minority displayed overt rejection (about one in ten in this instance) and felt that the local residents are under no obligation to assist the process of integration or to accept the peculiarities and outside loyalties of immigrants.

All informants (65)	
	%
Minorities have obligation to integrate	48
Local people should help	87
Local groups should help	88
Local people should tolerate peculiarities	90

But although there is a recognition that immigrants should be assisted in the process of integration, the methods respondents wished to employ amounted in practice to the placing of responsibility for action in the hands of the local authority – in particular the Housing and Education Departments. The duty of the people, it was strongly implied, lies in passive cooperation in the carrying-out of these policies. This assessment can be linked to attitudes on the part of respondents to local government. There was strong resistance to the suggestion that problems like immigration could be better handled if larger local government units were introduced. On the contrary, both members and non-members considered that the powers of existing local authorities should be increased. Moreover, there was a general feeling that the community was well served under existing arrangements by its elected councillors and local government officials – a view shared by non-politicians.

	All informants (65) %	Politicians (34) %	Non-politicians (31) %
Councillors			
Well served	60	67	52
Not well served	28	24	32
Don't know, etc.	12	9	16
Officials			
Well served	62	58	65
Not well served	20	27	13
Don't know, etc.	18	15	22

Informants were also asked to comment upon the value to the community of its Members of Parliament, its clergy, and its local businessmen. The MPs were particularly well rated, being thought to serve the community well by three in four informants. The local clergy and businessmen were rated roughly on a par with councillors and local officials.

	All informants (65) %	Politicians (34) %	Non-politicians (31) %
MP			
Well served	77	85	68
Not well served	5	6	3
Don't know, etc.	18	9	29
Clergy			
Well served	64	59	67
Not well served	21	32	10
Don't know, etc.	15	9	23
Businessmen			
Well served	56	62	48
Not well served	27	26	29
Don't know, etc.	17	12	23

A striking feature of the response of the members was that attitudes were bipartisan; that is, respondents from both major parties among the councillors responded favourably to the Member from the opposition party.

When asked about the extent to which individuals could exert influence on matters of public importance, the respondents were strongly inclined to stress the orthodox channels of communication – for example letters to local councillors, to the Members of Parliament, or to the local press. About half of the non-politicians in the sample felt that membership of a political party could increase the individual's influence by putting him in touch with the formal political structure. Only 3 of the 65 informants did not feel that political parties performed a useful function, and the generally favourable attitude towards politics was also reflected in the answer to a projective question: if the informant had a child interested in a political career, would he encourage or discourage this interest? Only six informants said they would discourage such interest.

Finally, respondents were asked about the extent to which they believed their views to be representative. The majority of informants felt in agreement on local issues with workmates, friends, family, and the political party they supported:

	Agree %	Disagree %	Don't know or not answered %
Workmates, members of same profession	69	17	14
Friends	71	5	24
Family	75	3	22
Political party	45	6	49

The level of perceived agreement with public opinion was, however, much lower, particularly among non-politicians. Among the politicians, the results were not affected by party affiliations.

The level of perceived disagreement with public opinion – particularly marked among the non-politicians – was not, however, as striking as it might appear. The majority who felt that they disagreed with public opinion often did so on the grounds that there was no public opinion with which to agree: the public was seen as apathetic and complacent.

	All informants (65) %	Politicians (34) %	Non-politicians (31) %
Agree	37	47	27
Disagree	40	38	42
Don't know	23	15	31

As we have seen, the divergence perceived by the opinion leaders between their own views and those of their constituents does not seem to be reflected in the response of the main sample, despite their greater readiness to stigmatize the newcomers as failing to contribute to the host society. Perhaps the most striking of all the findings in the main study is the limited extent to which respondents are concerned by the problems raised by immigration. Although, when invited to make an assessment of the situation, 49 per cent of the sample felt that local attitudes towards coloured people were less favourable than the national average, and 65 per cent (by far the highest level in any of the boroughs studied) felt that the situation was bound to deteriorate, when invited to assess the importance of the issue to themselves as individuals, only 38 per cent of those questioned regarded the immigration issue as being important or very important. Forty-three per cent felt that it was a matter of no great importance and 19 per cent that it was not important at all. It is against the background of these findings that the statement by one of the local Members should be seen:

> 'For over 10 years, from about 1954 to 1966, Commonwealth immigration was the principal, and at times the only, political issue in my constituency' (Powell 1967).

Can an issue that is neither the main preoccupation of the majority of local inhabitants nor one that finds expression through the orthodox channels of communication legitimately be described as the principal local political issue?

CONCLUSIONS

To sum up: although too many pieces are missing from the jigsaw to make up a complete picture, the outlines seem clear. A ground swell of anxiety existed in the area for some time, although its intensity has been exaggerated by stereotypes of the local situation largely derived from reports in the national mass media, which came to be accepted locally. This anxiety has been perceived by local politicians and other opinion-formers, but their initial response was to decline to participate in direct discussion of the issue. Instead, the subject was debated, when it was debated at all, in the context of broader issues, like that of housing. (One exception to this general rule has been the statements of the Medical Officer of Health, over time, on such matters as the immigrant birth-rate). In declining to discuss the issue as such, local opinion leaders acted in line with the national norm then prevailing; the reluctance of politicians to embark on such debate survived the controversial election campaign of 1964 in Smethwick. In general, local opinion leaders have preferred in the past to place their faith in existing institutions and invest confidence in their Members' capacity to represent their interest at Westminster. In these circumstances, public opinion was reflected neither in the local political debate nor in the public statements made at Westminster.

However, when the Member is prepared, as both the Wolverhampton Members have become in the period since the study was conducted, to give open expression to what they perceive as the anxieties and resentments of the local inhabitants, the barrier to the expression of hostile views is broken. It then becomes possible for councillors to say, as one member of Wolverhampton Council has recently done, that solutions are to be found only in some form of segregation.[5] The inertia of institutions and the willingness of those who participate in local political activities to assent to a conspiracy of silence on major issues can, it seems, be broken if an initiative is taken from above. Whether the situation produced as a result of such initiative is any more accurate a reflection of the desires of the majority of the local population than was the inertia that preceded it is, however, an open question.

Notes

1 The questionnaire was drafted by Mr John Bochel who also helped with the interviewing, together with Mr Alan Ball and Mr Colin McQuillan. Mr Robert Williams gathered background material and wrote a paper on housing conditions; Mr Michael Collins carried out the preliminary analysis. I am grateful to all of them and also to Mr Bochel and Mr John Dearlove for helpful criticism of earlier drafts.
2 MS. prepared for opinion leader study by Robert Williams.
3 These events took place before the passing of the Race Relations Act, 1968.
4 All quotations in this section are from the interview schedules.
5 'Integration is an evil system' declared Conservative Councillor Frank Wandsworth. He said that Wolverhampton Corporation should set an example, by introducing 'voluntary segregation' (Report in *Birmingham Post*, 8 May 1968).

References

ABRAMS, MARK 1969. The Incidence of Race Prejudice in England. In *Colour and Citizenship*, E. J. B. Rose and associates. London: Oxford University Press.

BURNEY, ELIZABETH 1968. *Housing on Trial*. London: Oxford University Press.

JONES, G. W. 1969. *Borough Politics*. London: Macmillan.

MOORHOUSE, GEOFFREY 1968. Article on Wolverhampton in *Guardian*, 4 May 1968.

POWELL, J. ENOCH 1967. Review Article in *Daily Telegraph*, 16 February 1967.

WEST MIDLANDS REGIONAL STUDY 1965. London: H.M. Stationery Office.

HAROLD WOLPE

Industrialism and Race in South Africa

INTRODUCTION

The emergence in South Africa of an advanced industrial economy
(Hobart Houghton 1964)[1] has provided the basis for the propositions which have become central to much of the recent analysis
of that society.

In brief, the thesis asserts that there is a contradiction between
economy and polity, between the processes of industrialization
and the (racial) political system. According to one version of the
thesis, the 'logical imperatives' of industrialization will transcend
the contradiction by urging '. . . the polity forward beyond its
[racial] ideology' (Horwitz 1967: 427). According to a second
version, the power of the polity to resist and even mould the economic pressures that are contradictory to it will result in a revolutionary struggle by the non-white masses (Asherson 1969: 55).

The main purpose of this paper is to examine some of the implications and limitations of the propositions common to both
versions, but, before doing so, it is necessary to set out the argument more fully. At the end of the paper an alternative approach
will be briefly considered.

INDUSTRIALIZATION AND RACE: THE INDUSTRIALISM
ARGUMENT

It is a familiar contention that there are certain inherent tendencies
in the processes of industrialization that press forward to dissolve
all traditional relations and make irrelevant all criteria (such as
race or colour) that are extraneous to the logic of these processes.

The main elements of this argument may be summarized as follows.[2] Industrialization involves both a changing division of labour, which is associated with technological advance, and increasing complexity in the allocation of resources to production. Both these factors induce a rational perspective on the participants in industry. This is so because, given these conditions, at least two requirements have to be fulfilled in order to achieve successful and efficient, that is profitable, industrial production. First, industrial manpower must be selected and utilized, not in terms of ascribed criteria, but in terms of technical qualifications for the job; and, second, the location of plants and the utilization of resources generally must be determined, not by political or ideological considerations, but by the 'needs' of industrial production.

The consequence of the pressures brought into play by the attempt to actualize these rational imperatives is that there are produced the conditions required for their fulfilment. These conditions, towards which industrial societies strain, include the following interrelated characteristics:

1 An impersonal labour market in which employers are able to employ, unconstrained by non-rational pressures, those who fit the requirements of productive efficiency; a high degree of labour mobility enabling employees to move to the areas where their particular skills are required; an adequate supply of trained labour, which involves making education and training available to all those with the requisite ability (whatever other characteristics they may possess); a system of allocating rewards for work strictly on the basis of skill and performance.

2 A high degree of mobility of physical resources and capital.

The antithesis of the integrative, universalistic rationality of the economy is found in the particularistic irrationality of race prejudice.[3]

Race prejudice includes a set of judgements or prejudgements about the inferiority of a socially defined racial group and its incapacity to perform certain roles appropriate to a particular society, beliefs about the undesirability and impossibility of the members of that racial group exercising authority, and various ideas related to social distance.

It seems clear that, if economic action is determined by these prejudices rather than by rational criteria, there would be no impersonal 'colour-blind' market for labour – employment would be based on racial criteria and not on qualifications and experience. Access to training and, therefore, mobility would be determined not by ability but by racial group membership. Similarly, racial and not economic criteria would determine mobility of resources and capital investment.

According to the industrialism thesis, as the economic system acts to dissolve racial criteria of action, the political system counter-acts to enforce them. That is to say, the attempt to actualize racial policies brings the political system into (ever sharper) contradiction[4] with the economy.

In a more or less systematic form these notions have been in-corporated into the analysis of South African society with which I am concerned here (Van den Berghe 1967; Horwitz 1967; Asherson 1969; Van der Horst 1965; Hutt 1964).[5]

The contradiction, it is argued, has been present throughout the development of industrialization in South Africa, but, hitherto, the racial values of the political system have dominated over the economy:

'. . . the South African economy of the 1960's has been de-cisively shaped, and perhaps determined, not merely by the kind of political intervention and increased government activities, which are the common experience of most countries of the western world, but by an overpowering pursuit of ideas, or ideology. . . . The polity has always sought its ideal and ideology – the White man's supremacy. The network of economic development had to follow accordingly' (Horwitz 1967: 10–11, 12).

However, today, while the policies of apartheid, articulated in the political system, are intended precisely to continue to mould the 'logical imperatives' of the economy to the pattern of racial discrimination and stratification, the powerful thrust of industrialization asserts itself increasingly against racial ideology (Asherson 1969: 57–8; Van der Horst 1965: 101; Van den Berghe 1967: 80).

In what form does the contradiction appear? Three different formulations are discernible in the literature. The first of these asserts that the contradiction is between the *fact* of increasing participation of all races in a single, increasingly industrial, economic system and the *formal* ideology of apartheid, in so far as the latter prescribes total geographical separation of the races in South Africa. Since, apart from its doubtful relevance to the industrialism thesis, there is no empirical evidence whatsoever of an intended or unintended tendency towards total geographical separation, this contradiction is merely formal and as such will not be dealt with further.

The second formulation asserts that the fact of increasing mutual economic involvement exerts also an integrative force outside the economy which contradicts the pressures of apartheid policies towards political, residential, and social segregation and inequality in the non-economic sectors (Van den Berghe 1967: 272–4; Van der Horst 1965: 101). Leaving aside the obvious fact that the trend has been towards greater, not less, residential and social segregation and fewer, not more, political rights, it is difficult to see why mere involvement in the economic system should produce the suggested consequences. The notion becomes more meaningful in the third formulation.

In its third form the contradiction is said to be between the equalizing pressures of the processes of industrialization and the politically maintained racial inequalities within the economic system, although, ultimately economic racial equality, it is argued, will penetrate into the political and social sectors also. Concretely, the contradiction manifests itself in the struggle to maintain the system of cheap black labour which is gradually, but inevitably, disintegrating under the impetus of industrial development; and, second, in the attempt to block both the gradual, equally inevitable, 'encroachment' of blacks into education, training, and skilled jobs, and also the replacement of ascriptive racial criteria by other criteria of job placement. The explanation of the tendencies of the economic system lies in the fact that, first, the cheap labour system is wasteful socially as well as economically and, in addition, by keeping wages low, inhibits the development of a home market thereby depressing the profitability of the economy; second, the exclusion of blacks from training, etc., results in extreme shortages of needed manpower.

It seems to be a necessary implication of the above argument that, 'left to itself', the industrial productive system would tend to dissolve pre-existing racial discrimination and inhibit any further development of it, not only within the economy, but also in the political and social systems of the society. This leads to two further conclusions. First, to the degree to which racial discrimination exists and persists in the economic structure, it must be held to have been imposed from 'outside' this structure by non-economic pressures; and, second, racial discrimination in the political and social structures must likewise be due to non-economic factors. The question that now arises is: how is racial discrimination to be accounted for? The answers that the industrialism thesis gives to this question flow directly from two underlying assumptions that are essential to the whole argument and that have thus far remained implicit in the discussion. One assumption is that the economic and political/social systems can be analysed as relatively autonomous 'entities', which impinge upon one another only in so far as each constitutes part of the external environment of the other. The second assumption is that the action of actors is satisfactorily explained by a description of the values, beliefs, ideas, etc., that are assumed to 'cause' them to act in a particular way.

These assumptions enter into the analysis of South African society in two different ways. On the one hand, since racial ideas and discriminatory actions are asserted to have their origin and *raison d'être* in the political system, the structure and processes of the economic system are excluded from the explanation of the genesis and operation of racial discrimination. On the other hand, the 'rational imperatives' of the industrial system are analysed as if the content of rationality can be arrived at abstractly, 'uncontaminated' by the existing ideologies, class structure, and political system.

It is now possible to consider to what extent this approach

F

provides a satisfactory basis for the analysis of South African society.

A CRITIQUE OF THE INDUSTRIALISM ARGUMENT

Race Prejudice as the Cause of Discrimination

As I have already indicated, the industrialism thesis asserts that the imposition of racial discrimination in the economy is due to racial beliefs (prejudice or ideology) emanating and operating 'outside' the economic system, but impinging upon the latter. That is to say, race prejudice is said to be the cause of racial discrimination. MacCrone, in a different context, has expressed this as follows:

'. . . the Native problem is, in terms of the underlying psychological realities, a problem in the mind of the white man since it is the problem created and constituted by the race attitudes and colour prejudices or, in other words, by the caste attitudes, of the members of an upper caste in a colour-caste society' (MacCrone 1947: 30).[6]

While a number of refinements concerning the differential operation of prejudice in changing circumstances are sometimes introduced into the discussion, prejudice is, nevertheless, maintained to be the causal factor that accounts for the relationships. In sum, a member of a racial group is treated unequally, it is asserted, because he is defined as a member of that group.[7]

This would seem to give rise to questions concerning the conditions in which such definitions or attitudes of hostility arise but, in fact, sociologists who adopt this approach simply take these as given and, as a consequence, race relations are removed from both an economic and political structural context and treated as an area *sui generis*.[8] Since it *is* taken as given, the need to account for race prejudice in structural terms does not arise and all that is then considered necessary is a description of its consequences.[9] It is of interest to note that by focusing in this way on race prejudice (or attitudes or ideology) the sociologist adopts the actors' definition of the situation as the basis of his explanation. Since this definition must involve also a delineation of what is considered relevant to action, its incorporation by the sociologist into his analytical framework involves simultaneously an acceptance of the social definition of relevance and, therefore, the exclusion from the analysis of other factors considered by the actors to be irrelevant.

While a structure of legitimation may be one of the conditions of action, it cannot be assumed that it encompasses all that is relevant or that it is the cause of action. For one thing, the emergence of such a structure is related to the patterns of economic and political power. The transformation of the Calvinism of the Dutch settlers into a racial ideology in the conditions of a frontier society in South Africa is a case in point (MacCrone 1947; Tiryakian 1957: 342). For another thing, general ideological principles and generalized racial prejudices are never 'applied' abstractly, they have always to be interpreted in concrete situations that condition the interpretations. The 'bending' of the racial prejudice to meet recurring political and economic exigencies is illustrated by reference to the system of 'job reservation' by which occupations are defined as black or white in South Africa.

By 1920 it had become accepted by the white workers in the gold-mines that no non-white could work without white supervision, that there should be a fixed ratio of whites to non-whites, and that skilled and semi-skilled jobs were to be the preserve of white workers. The Chamber of Mines, however, was faced with rising costs but no corresponding increase in the price of gold. This affected the level of profit, tended to make the mining of low-grade ores uneconomical from the point of view of the Chamber, and thus raised the possibility that the Chamber would close down some mines unless a reorganization was effected. As Doxey (1961: 24) put it:

'The main problem of costs lay in the field of labour and in particular the cost of white labour. Whereas African wages had only risen 9 per cent since before the War (1914–1918), European wages rose by about 60 per cent between 1913 and 1918. In the circumstances it was natural that the companies should have sought to solve their problem by reorganisation.'

What was the envisaged reorganization? The Chamber planned, *inter alia*, to employ Africans in semi-skilled jobs previously reserved for white workers. The white workers responded by launching a strike in 1922 which developed into a general strike and culminated in the 'Rand Revolt'. The strikers raised the slogan 'Workers of the World Unite and Fight for a White South Africa'. Although the latter half of the slogan is always pointed to as proof of the fact that the strike was caused by racial prejudice, what tends to be overlooked is the context in which the strike took place. There are three relevant factors. First, there were some 200,000 unemployed 'poor whites' out of a total white population of about one and a half million; second, notwithstanding public declarations (by whites) to the effect that Africans were only capable of unskilled work, large numbers of African mine-workers were acquiring skills in the mines and were, in fact, carrying out most operations (including those which were supposed to be the preserve of white skilled workers) unsupervised; third, the Chamber of Mines (supported by the findings of various government commissions) was intent, not only upon employing African workers in 'white' jobs, but also upon employing them at lower wages than were paid to whites. Although the strike was broken, the Chamber did not introduce the intended changes. A similar attempt by the Chamber in the 1960s, it should be noted, was again blocked by the white mine-workers.

In 1956 the Industrial Conciliation Act was amended to give the government unrestricted legal power to reserve jobs for particular racial groups. Notwithstanding this, it is clear that in conditions of economic expansion and a shortage of skilled and semi-skilled white workers, Africans are increasingly being employed in semi-skilled and clerical jobs that were previously the monopoly of white workers. An illuminating case in point is the employment of Africans in semi-skilled or clerical work in the state-run postal service and railways (Horrell 1965: 212).

In what sense can the above facts be explained simply by asserting race prejudice as the cause? In some occupational sectors black labour is strictly confined to unskilled manual work, while in others black labour is admitted to semi-skilled and white-collar work (including work previously reserved for white labour). To assert that prejudice is the cause in both cases is to explain nothing – at best it amounts to a redescription of the original facts in different words. But what needs to be explained is the differential position of the two categories of African workers. What is patent is that in each case certain structural conditions determined the action and have to be taken into account in the analysis.

This latter point can be made more generally by an examination of Van den Berghe's approach. He says:

'Of greater interest yet is the lack of salience of social class in South Africa. To be sure, there exist income and occupational strata within each of the four races, but at the same time, there is a high correlation between socio-economic variables and race. Social classes in the Marxian sense of relationship to the means of production exist by definition, as they must in any capitalist country, but they are not meaningful social realities. Clearly, pigmentation, rather than ownership of land or capital, is the most significant criterion of status in South Africa' (Van den Berghe 1967: 267).

It seems clear from the passage cited that in explaining the position of, and relationships between, social groups, class is made irrelevant and socio-economic differentials are treated as the outcome of racial definitions. Now, since pigmentation is the significant factor and since, furthermore, pigmentation is only relevant in that it is '. . . seized upon . . . as a [criterion] of group definition' (Van den Berghe 1967: 266), it follows that the situation of particular groups is determined by the way they are defined by others. More specifically, that is, the relationships between social groups must be seen as solely a function of racial ideology, attitudes, and prejudices.

If the existence is assumed of a common value system in terms of which non-whites concur in the ideology of race prejudice, then there is no further problem.[10] Not only is this an assumption which cannot be made of South Africa (if indeed it can ever be made of any society), but Van den Berghe (1967: 4) specifically asserts the contrary: 'More abstractly, South Africa is ridden with almost total lack of consensus of values, i.e. on what its people consider desirable goals to achieve.'

But if there is no consensus about values, how is the pattern of group relations to be explained? Here Van den Berghe, in the concluding pages of his book, briefly suggests three different bases – compliance, coercion, and economic dependence. Each of these is involved in and arises from a structure of economic and political power. Economic dependence is the most important aspect, according to Van den Berghe (1967: 274).

'The utter dependence (at a starvation or near starvation level) of the African masses on the "White" economy, has been one of the main inhibiting factors to such mass protest action as general strikes.'

Thus, having dismissed the relevance of 'Marxist classes', the analysis is forced to return to some such notion by the back door. This both points to the inadequacy of attempting to separate 'race relations' from an analysis of the structures and processes that are relevant to an investigation of any aspect of society, and more specifically emphasizes the need *systematically* to investigate the interrelationship between race prejudice and political and economic structures.

The point can be further illustrated by reference to political analyses that make assumptions similar to those I have been considering. Horwitz's (1967) analysis of the political aims and objectives of the Afrikaners will serve as an example. He contends that, in pursuing policies of racial discrimination from 'outside' the economy, the purpose was only to preserve an existing, superior political and social status. That is to say, the economic-class implications of such a policy are ignored. This view can perhaps be accounted for by the fact that the most rigorous and extreme formulations of race prejudice were made precisely by those white strata of different classes who were outside of the centres of economic power. These were the unemployed 'poor white' stratum of the working class, on the one hand, and the Afrikaner farmers, on the other hand. The latter constituted the weakest sector of the capitalist class, unable to penetrate the economically powerful gold and diamond mine monopolies or finance, banking, insurance, and industry, all of which were controlled by foreign or local 'English' capital.

Horwitz (1967: 166) characterizes the purposes of Afrikaner-doms' struggle for a racial polity as follows:

'The electoral weight of rural Afrikanerdom was deployed to secure control of the polity of Afrikanerdom, so that Afrikaner nationalism might direct the executive and administrative authority within the polity to shape the adaptive compulsions of economic rationality.'

The passage suggests, and indeed the whole of Horwitz's book argues, that the Afrikaner nationalists' struggle was to control the economy from a position of political power, but only for the limited objective of ensuring that the economy did not undermine white social and political supremacy. Because of this, no adequate analysis is made of the relationship between class relations and political and economic conflict. However, in the course of a discussion on the Afrikaner nationalists' attempt to develop a protective *culture* defence against economic change, Horwitz presents some evidence of the economic aspects of the political struggle without apparently realizing the contradictory implications of this evidence for his thesis.

He states that in 1929 the 'Broederbond', a powerful secret organization of Afrikaner nationalism, established the 'Federasie van Afrikaanse Kultuurvereeninging' (Federation of Afrikaans Cultural Organizations: FAK). This body in turn established various economic, financial, and commercial organizations. In particular the 'Reedingsdaabond' (RDB) was established with the explicit purpose of training the Afrikaner people to 'take their place' in industrial society and to mobilize 'the capital resources of the Afrikaner people'. In this, the RDB proved very effective, leading to the establishment of Afrikaner-controlled banks, building societies, and other financial institutions, which developed 'a self-generating' growth of capital (Horwitz 1967: 270–1). The outcome had predictable ideological consequences. As Horwitz (1967: 408) states:

'It is striking from 1948 onwards, when capital formation among Afrikaners went ahead rapidly often aided by the inter-connections with political Afrikanerdom, now in indisputable command of the polity, that industrialization and profit making capitalistic enterprise became not only highly respectable but patriotic.'

The inappropriateness of attempting to analyse South African social relationships solely in terms of racial ideologies or prejudices is again apparent.

Differing Notions of Racial Discrimination

To a considerable extent this tendency to focus on racial ideology as the given, unproblematical cause of racial discrimination flows directly from the way in which the latter is conceptualized. That is to say, by assuming that the differential position of particular groups is due to race prejudice, there is excluded from the analysis discrimination that is either economically motivated, or arises in or through the operation of the economic system, or that is a consequence of a particular distribution of power, or, in any event, is not caused by race prejudice. There is, however, an alternative way of conceptualizing discrimination that avoids this arbitrary exclusion.

In one sense of discrimination there may be an intention to discriminate, but it does not follow from this that intention is to be identified with cause. Thus, if an industrial enterprise that employs a number of workers on identical work pays the black workers half as much as the white workers, there may be an intention to discriminate against the black workers, but this does not imply that it is due to racial prejudice. The explanation of the discrimination would require an analysis not only of the ideational factors but also of the political and economic context within which it occurs – including the relative power position of black workers *vis-à-vis* the white workers.

A considerable amount of discrimination in South Africa is intentional – in fact, all discriminatory legislation falls into this category. But neither the cause nor the significance of this intentional discrimination can be uncovered by examining each discriminatory law or Act and asserting that it is due to prejudice. What is required is a framework of analysis within which acts of discrimination can be accounted for and understood as the outcome of the interrelationship of a configuration of factors in a social structure.

A second type of discrimination of at least equal importance can be referred to as structural discrimination. It is this type of discrimination which Stokeley Carmichael (1968: 151–2) presumably had in mind in the following passage:

'When . . . white terrorists bomb a black church and kill five black children, that is an act of individual racism. . . . But when in that same city, Birmingham, Alabama, not 5 but 500 black babies die each year because of lack of proper food, shelter and medical facilities; and thousands more are destroyed and maimed physically, emotionally and intellectually because of conditions of poverty and discrimination in the black community, that is a function of institutionalized racism. . . . It is institutionalized racism that keeps the black people locked in dilapidated slums, tenements, where they must hire out their daily lives subject to the prey of exploiting slum landlords, merchants, loan-sharks and the restrictive practices of real estate agents.'[11]

The point about this type of structural discrimination is that it is not confined to coloured people in racially mixed societies. I showed this when earlier I referred to the immense number of 'poor whites' (impoverished rural migrants) in South Africa who were subject to precisely the same type of pressure that drove black people into the urban areas. This, of course, is not to contend that there are no inequalities between black and white people in South Africa. On the contrary, the inequalities are vast and increasing.[12] But this fact must not be allowed to confuse the analysis or drive us to simplistic assumptions about the cause of these inequalities.

This argument is reinforced by the obvious fact that social, political, and economic differentials are not found only in racially mixed societies – impoverished, unskilled, and disadvantaged strata are to be found in other societies including advanced industrial societies. What is relevant in the present context is that *one* of the important respects in which these societies are differentiated from a racially mixed society such as South Africa is by the content of the legitimating beliefs that sanction the inequalities. Poverty is not a function of race or colour, it is the outcome of the actions of men pursuing economic ends in specific social structures.

The 'Logical Imperatives' of Industrialization in Relation to Race

In the previous sections I tried to show that only by adopting a particular, unsatisfactory, causal theory was it possible to maintain the view that racial discrimination is generated and maintained exclusively or, at least, overwhelmingly by ideological factors outside the economic system. I now want to examine the other aspect of the industrialism thesis, namely, the argument that the industrial system, by its nature, is antithetical to racial discrimination. In doing so, it is not my intention to make an extended analysis or criticism of the industrialism thesis but only to consider two aspects of it.

The point has frequently been made that there are no good grounds for making the general assumption that industrialization will necessarily have an eroding effect upon traditional institutions or upon relations that are said to be irrational from the point of view of a supposed economic rationality.[13]

Blumer (1965: 240–1) has argued, specifically with regard to race relations, that there is no evidence at all to suggest that the industrializing process has had a dissolving effect upon these relations.

'The most outstanding observation that is forced upon us by empirical evidence is that the apparatus and operations introduced by industrialization almost invariably adjust and conform to the pattern of race relations in the given society.'

In parenthesis it is of interest to note that this leads Blumer to the conclusion that change in the industrial pattern of race stratification will have to be brought about by pressures originating in the political structure.

Kuper (1965: 45–6), similarly, has contended that the economy utilizes existing stratification patterns:

'Indeed, racial stratification in South Africa may assist the process of integration, if integration is conceived as involving the precise interweaving of the parts into a functioning whole. Control over the movement of Africans, the systems of influx and efflux control and of Labour bureaux, permits, in theory, the exact integration of African labour into the economy. African labour . . . can be fed into the economy in the precise quantities and qualities desired without any redundancies in the urban areas. Surplus workers will move out of sight into the reserves to provide a labour pool for new or changing demands, and their poverty will not be a charge on the industrial areas.'

Perhaps, however, it is more important to consider the content of the notion of economic rationality, at least as it has been elaborated in the South African context. In relation to labour, the assumption is that the crucially relevant condition for the actualization of rational economic action in production is the supply, on the impersonal market, of the required number of adequately trained workers. But this is only one relevant factor. In making rational decisions in specific conditions, other conditions have to be weighed too. Blumer (1965: 233) has pointed to one example:

'. . . the rational or secular perspective, which industrialism admittedly fosters and stresses, may compel an adherence to the racial system rather than a departure from it. The manager of an industrial plant who may be willing to hire workers of a subordinate racial group . . . may definitely refrain from doing so in order not to provoke difficulties with other workers. This is a *rational* decision . . .'

The cost of labour is, of course, another crucial factor in rational economic calculation. The mechanism whereby the supply of low-cost labour is obtained in South Africa is the cheap-labour system of which Pass Laws and migrant labour are important elements. However, as I have already pointed out, it is argued that this system (one of the main manifestations of the differential position of the races) is irrational from the point of the economic system, since it is wasteful socially and economically and impedes the development of internal markets. This system, the argument continues, is maintained, *inter alia*, by the imposition of obstacles in the way of Africans receiving education and training. This, too, is irrational from the perspective of the economy, since it results in gross manpower shortages (Horrell 1965: 208),[14] which impede economic growth. The development of a highly industrialized economic system exerts pressures to corrode the cheap-labour system and obstacles to training, but this brings it into conflict with the 'external' racial pressures.

This belief that there is a contradiction between the industrializing process and racial discrimination is based upon the further assumption that there is a contradiction between the production of a more highly skilled African industrial labour force and the maintenance of the supply of low-cost African labour. But this assertion fails to take account of the mechanisms by which it is possible simultaneously to increase supplies of trained labour and maintain low labour costs – mechanisms that are not, of course, restricted to South Africa.

Thus in South Africa there are innumerable examples of African workers performing skilled and semi-skilled work, in occupations from which they have been excluded by law or by industrial agreements between white workers and employers, at wages well below those fixed for whites.[15]

The processes of job dilution and job redefinition, however, are the main mechanisms in this context. In discussing this in relation to South Africa, we may begin with the Bantu Education Act. It has usually been emphasized that the purpose of this Act was to ensure the 'proper' indoctrination of Africans to accept their subservient position. In support of this view, it has been pointed out that private education of Africans (by missionaries or otherwise) was proscribed (except under permit) and that control of African education generally was taken out of the hands of the provincial governments and placed under the control of the central government's Department of Bantu Affairs. In addition, supporting evidence has been cited from statements by members of the government. Dr Verwoerd, for example, said of the purpose of the Act:

> 'Education must train and teach people, in accordance with their opportunities in life, according to the sphere in which they live. Good race relations cannot exist where education is given under the control of people who create the wrong expectations on the part of the native himself. . . . *Native education should be controlled in such a way that it should be in accordance with the policy of the State* . . .'[16] (emphasis added).

There is no doubt that the interpretation given to the Act is correct so far as it goes. At the same time, it is important to note that the number of African children receiving *some* education rose very sharply after the introduction of the Act. This is so not only in absolute numbers, but also in terms of the proportion of school-goers to the total African population, the increase in the latter being from approximately 1 in 11 to about 1 in 6.[17]

It seems significant that this increase should have coincided with the growing demand for workers with some training that resulted from the rapid development of the industrial and commercial sector of the economy as well as the railways, communications, and so on. But the equally significant point here is that, simultaneously, processes of dilution and redefinition have occurred allowing Africans, despite the existence of legal provisions empowering the government to enforce the contrary, to take over white jobs or enter semi-skilled work at low rates of pay. While this aspect requires to be fully investigated, there is already considerable evidence indicating the trends in a variety of industries (Doxey 1961: 191–4; Horrell 1969: 88–126). It is, perhaps, safe to predict that, although the pace will vary according to the conditions in particular industries, the process will tend to accelerate as the demand for trained labour intensifies in an expanding economy.

Cheap Labour and the South African Economy

The inadequacy of the contention that there is a contradiction between the economy and the racial polity is revealed, above all, by the critical importance of low-cost black labour to the rational (i.e. profitable) conduct of the South African economy. Far from economic discrimination being 'foreign' to the economy, it has its origins in economic activity and it is maintained both by the economic structure and, as the industrialism thesis argues, by the political structure.

What is meant by cheap labour can be seen from a rather abbreviated comparison of wages in various sectors of the economy. The following tables show the average annual cash wages for whites and Africans in mining and manufacturing in three different years.

Average Annual Cash Wages in Pounds[18]

	Mining				Manufacturing and construction			
	At current prices		At 1959 prices		At current prices		At 1959 prices	
	Whites	*Non-whites**	*Whites*	*Non-whites*	*Whites*	*Africans*	*Whites*	*Africans*
1938	384	34	858	75	246	47	500	105
1946	534	44	884	73	425	100	696	164
1960	1164	71	1146	70	964	185	903	182
1967	1692	108 (approx.)			1524	258		

* Although the figures refer to non-whites generally the overwhelming majority of non-white employees in the mines are Africans.

It can be seen from the above table that the gap between African and white wages has tended to increase, particularly in the mining industry. However, the main point is that African cash wages have tended to remain at about one-sixteenth of white wages in the mining industry and at about one-fifth or one-sixth of white wages in manufacturing and construction. In the case of mining, it has been estimated that if wages in kind (barrack housing, food, etc.) are taken into account non-white wages amount to one-ninth of white wages, but these figures have been challenged on the ground that they fail to take into account various deductions made by the mines from wages.

Doxey (1961: 183-4) has pointed out that in 1956 whites, who constituted 12 per cent of the mines' labour force, received 71 per cent of the total wages paid by the mines, whereas Africans, who constituted 88 per cent of the labour, were paid 29 per cent of the wages.

The situation in agriculture is similar – in 1953-4 the average annual wage for African agricultural labourers was £37 compared with £300 for whites.

The importance of cheap labour to 'white' agriculture, which, for a number of reasons, has had to be constantly subsidized by the government, and to a mining industry that is unable to exercise control over the price of gold on the international market, has been fully documented.[19] The major contribution that mining and farming make to the national income is indicated in the table in Note 1.

Under what conditions were Africans converted into a supply of cheap labour? Industrialization in South Africa begins with the discovery of diamonds (1867) and gold (1886). Africans became low-paid labourers in the mines, not because of the racial prejudices of the mine-owners, but because they were powerless economically and politically. They were 'pushed' into the mines by economic pressures – land shortage and exhaustion and poll taxes – and through recruiting agencies. Their lack of skill, their instability as a working class because of the migrant labour system, the absence of trade-union organization, and their very abundance laid them open to low wages.[20]

The vulnerability of Africans to low wages has been maintained by a complex of conditions that have ensured their relative powerlessness. Among these conditions are continuing rural underdevelopment in the African Reserves, the intricate system of labour-directing Pass Laws, the differential access to education and training, the system of migrant labour, the weakness of their trade unions and the strength of the white trade unions, and the power of capital. All this is, of course, underpinned by the white-dominated political structures.

Enough has been said, I suggest, to expose the inadequacy of attempting to treat 'race' as exogenous to the economic system or, in the South African situation, as contradictory to it. The analysis, then, has to be approached on a different basis, which not only relates 'race' to structural conditions but also accounts for the convergence of political and economic discrimination that sets the lines of conflict. One such approach has conceived of South African society in terms of 'internal colonialism'.

INTERNAL COLONIALISM

The term 'domestic' or 'internal' colonialism has been employed differently by a number of writers, but its analytical implications have not been systematically pursued.

Carter, Karis, and Stultz (1967: 42), for example, content themselves with describing the African Reserves (the so-called Bantustans) as domestic colonies which constitute: 'Mere sources of unskilled labour for the country's vigorous economy.'

Marquard (1957) outlines a different analysis. He suggests that colonial conquest may occur in one of two ways. In the first, of which pre-independence South Africa is an instance, the conquerors settle permanently in large number; in the second, there are a few temporary administrators, traders, and missionaries. In both cases, conquest involves annexation of the land and the 'double exploitation' of the indigenous people, 'once as labourer and once as native' (Marquard 1957: 2–3). Both features continued in South Africa with the establishment of the internal colonial structure upon the granting of independence in 1910. The effect was to raise: '. . . the status of the European colonists to that of rulers while it left four fifths of the population in the condition of colonial subjects' (Marquard 1957: 6).

The core feature of Marquard's analysis is that he assumes the relevant categories to be 'European Ruler' on the one side and the 'coloured subjects' on the other, and he takes the homogeneity of these categories for granted. As a consequence, he does not analyse the class relationships of the society or the class structure of either of his categories. This gives rise to the problems to which I drew attention earlier in the paper.

It is largely with respect to the analysis of class relations that the argument is extended, albeit not always consistently, in the South African Communist Party's (SACP 1962) document 'The Road to South African Freedom'. The analysis here runs as follows: With independence, power was transferred '. . . not into the hands of the masses of the people of South Africa, but into the hands of the white minority alone' (SACP 1962: 25).

But the white ruling group is not homogeneous. It is divided into two main classes – a capitalist class, consisting of the mining, banking, and financial monopolies together with large farmers and the owners of industrial enterprises, which exercises 'real power', and a white working class, which, although exploited, constitutes a 'labour aristocracy' (SACP 1962: 27). The development of capitalism in South Africa was based upon an abundant supply of cheap black labour, the flow of which was ensured by the under-development of the limited land available to Africans. Cheap labour is the source not only of immense profits, but also of the high wages and standard of living of the whites. The whole structure is maintained primarily by the 'national oppression' of the black people in all spheres of social life, through the exercise of state coercion supported by all sections of the white population. The convergence, albeit unevenly, of economic and political power-lessness with 'blackness', together with the legitimating racial ideology, gives the society its unique internal colonial nature, according to this view.

It is clear from this brief discussion of the internal colonialism thesis that it diverges markedly from the views discussed in the earlier sections of the paper. In particular, there is a shift from a purely attitudinal level of analysis to an analysis of the structural basis of both discrimination and racial ideology. In addition, for the contradictory relationship between an abstract economic rationality and racial ideology, there is substituted the conception of an economic system based on cheap labour as the key structuring 'part' of the system.

What is obviously involved here is an analysis of class structure and relationships. However, although for some purposes (particularly the characterization of the nature of the social system as a whole) it is possible to treat classes both in a general way and as if they were internally homogeneous, for other purposes this is quite inadequate. The reason why it is inadequate is that the relationship between classes is partly a function of the relationship of strata within classes, just as the relationship between strata is a function of the relationship between classes.

The point can be illustrated by a historical, but none the less interesting and relevant, example.

In the 1880s the diamond mine-owners, believing (rightly) that both white and African workers were stealing diamonds found by them on the diggings, attempted to institute a search of miners as they came off the diggings.

By this time skilled workers of British origin with trade-union experience were already being employed in the mines and they had organized a trade union of white workers. The unskilled black workers were, apparently, completely unorganized. One of the reasons for this was that they were migrant workers who remained no longer than three months at a time on the diggings. Although accuracy is impossible, one observer has estimated that while there were at most 20,000 African mineworkers at any one time (others put the figure at approximately 8,000) over 300,000 Africans worked on the diggings during the five-year period in the 1870s.

The white workers' trade union resisted the attempt to search their members. The workers held meetings, negotiated, and finally struck work and rioted. African workers were also opposed to being searched – they were discontented with a procedure that threatened an important source of income! This fact has tended to be overlooked, no doubt because African resistance did not manifest itself on the diggings (although some Africans supported the white rioters) but was expressed, it seems, by the simple expedient of not going to the diggings to take up work (Doxey 1961: Ch. 2).

This difference in the mode of opposing the searching had important consequences. The white workers' struggle succeeded and, in succeeding, strengthened the cohesion of the workers and their organizational power. The resistance of African workers had no similar results. This differential in organizational strength was to have continuous repercussions in, for example, the struggle for higher wages. The relationship between white workers and mine-owners was always conditioned by the relative strength of the former and by the relative powerlessness of African workers resulting in an ever-increasing gap in wages between the two strata.

The implications of this illustration are that the relationships between racial groups in South Africa must be analysed in terms of the ongoing relationships of strata and classes, which are structured in terms of differential access to resources, organization, skills, status, and so on.

In another context, Frank (1967: 9) has appositely expressed a similar approach as follows:

'Economic development and underdevelopment are not just relative and quantitative . . . they are relational and qualitative, in that each is structurally different from, yet caused by its relations with, the others. Yet development and underdevelopment are the same in that they are the product of a single but dialectically contradictory, economic structure and process of capitalism.'

A comprehensive analysis of South African society from this perspective, which still remains to be made, would involve the systematic elaboration of the concept of internal colonialism of which the barest outlines have been given in this paper.

CONCLUSION

In the introduction to this paper I referred to two different views about the way in which the asserted contradiction between the economy and the racial political structure was likely to be resolved. The first, which contends that the very pressure of economic development will result in the reformation of the society, has in fact been dealt with. The second view holds that the contradiction will persist until political action by the non-white masses terminates the racial order through the conquest of power.[21]

The basis of this conclusion seems to be the belief that the contradiction will generate conflict between white and black because, presumably, of the continuing incapacity of the economy, constrained by 'external' racialism, to satisfy the economic requirements of the non-white people. Against this latter point I have argued, by implication, that the relative impoverishment and, therefore, powerlessness of the non-white people is a condition of the continued development of the existing economy of South Africa and it follows, therefore, that the contradiction must be sought in a different set of relationships from those suggested by the industrialism thesis. Be that as it may, it is clear that the analysis of the structural position of particular groups and the contradictory processes that tend to generate conflict between them does not of itself reveal how the political conflict will in fact develop. For this we need to examine other, additional, factors that are, however, beyond the scope of this paper.

Notes

1 The nature and extent of the relevant changes can be sufficiently indicated by reference to the statistics of national income and urbanization which have been compiled from various sources.

The national income increased from £395,000,000 in 1939 to £2,500,000 million in 1961–2. The figures for the percentage contribution of different sectors of the economy to the national income show the typical shift in favour of industrial manufacture.

Contribution of different economic sectors to the
national income
(Millions of pounds)

Year	Agriculture and Forestry		Mining		Private manufacture		Commerce and Trade		Public Authorities and others	
	£	%	£	%	£	%	£	%	£	%
1911–12	23	17·4	36	27·1	8·9	6·7	18	13·5	47	35·3
1938–9	51	12·8	82	20·6	70	17·7	54	13·6	139	35·3
1961–2	268	10·7	337	13·7	603	24·0	315	12·7	979	38·9

The increasing urbanization of the population is shown in the following table:

Percentage of each racial group in urban areas

	1936	1960
White	65·2	80
African	17·3	30
Coloured	53·9	63
Asians	66·3	80

2 For an extended discussion of the propositions summarized here, see among others Blumer (1965: 22), Kerr *et al.* (1960), Van den Berghe (1967), Horwitz (1967), Asherson (1969), Van der Horst (1965: 101), Hutt (1964).

3 Throughout the paper I use the terms race prejudice, attitude, and ideology interchangeably since my focus is on the ideational element as a causal factor in social action.

4 The term contradiction is used by the writers who have developed the 'theory' I am examining and I am, therefore, following their usage for the sake of convenience. It seems to me, however, that in fact the notion of 'dysfunction' would be more appropriate in this discussion since the effects of the political relations appear to be viewed from the perspective of the 'functional' requisites of the industrial order.

5 The argument is also considered in Kuper (1965: Chapter 5).

6 See also: Horwitz, op. cit., Asherson, op. cit., Dickie-Clark (1966).

7 For a similar argument, see Blalock (1967: 15).

8 This is so even though race prejudice is located in the political structure, since it is not explained in terms of this structure.

9 Which no doubt explains why the overwhelming bulk of the writing on race in South Africa is purely at the descriptive level – once, that is, the assumption of race prejudice as cause has been made.

10 I leave aside the difficulty that rises from the lack of consensus stemming from commitment to race prejudice, on the one hand, and economic rationality, on the other.

11 See also Hobart Houghton (1964: 160).

12 The South African population of 16 million is divided, in terms of the prevailing social and legal definitions, into four racial groups as follows:

> Africans: 11,000,000
> Whites: 3,000,000
> Coloureds: 1,500,000
> Asians: 500,000

The differential position of each of these groups and, in particular, the unequal situation of the three non-white groups by comparison with the white group, exists in respect of all socio-economic variables. This can be illustrated by a highly abridged reference to some of the relevant statistics taken from Horrell (1965 and 1968), Van den Berghe (1967).

TABLE I

	Africans	Asians and coloureds	Whites
Annual state expenditure for education per pupil (1962)	£6·4	£20 (est.)	£65
No. of students enrolled at universities (1965)	2,413	3,673	50,735
Per capita incomes (1960)	£43·5	£67·5	£476
% of national income received (1960) against % of total population constituted by each racial group	26·5	6·5	67
Average family income (1953–4)	£119·2	£308	£1,616

TABLE 2

School enrolment and distribution between primary and secondary school

	Total enrolment	% in primary school	% in secondary school
Africans (1963)	1,764,150	96·63	3·02
Whites (1963)	730,347	66·00	34·00
Coloureds (1964)	368,131	90·93	9·07
Asians (1962)	—	84·8	15·2

TABLE 3

Racial composition of various skill levels (1951)

	Skilled %	Semi-skilled %	Unskilled %
Africans	5	40	85
Coloureds and Asians	10	30	14
Whites	85	30	1
	100	100	100

TABLE 4

Percentage at various levels of skill of industrial workers of each race (1956)

	Africans %	Coloureds %	Asians %	Whites %
Skilled	5·2	19·2	38·6	86·4
Semi-skilled	15·0	30·1	30·2	12·5
Unskilled	79·8	50·7	31·2	1·1
	100	100	100	100

For detailed discussions of these and related aspects, see Horwitz (1967), Horrell (1965, 1968), Doxey (1961), Van der Horst (1942), Spooner (1960), from which the trend towards increasing differentials between black and white emerge.

13 See for example Budd and Platt (1964).
14 See also Educational Panel Report (1966).
15 See in this connection the extracts from Government commissions on the gold mines quoted by both Doxey (1961) and Horwitz (1967).
16 Quoted in the Second Report of the UN Committee on the Racial Situation in South Africa, (A/2719) paragraph 56.
17 As *Table 2* (Note 12) indicates, however, some 96 per cent of these are in primary schools.
18 Derived and abridged from Hobart Houghton (1964).
19 One of the best accounts is De Kiewiet (1942).
20 See De Kiewiet for a full account.
21 Horwitz (1967) takes the first line, Asherson (1969) and Van den Berghe (1967) the second.

ACKNOWLEDGEMENTS

I wish to thank Roy Bailey (now of the Department of Social Sciences, Enfield College of Technology) and Stewart Bentley, School of Social Sciences, University of Bradford, for comments and suggestions on earlier drafts of this paper.

References

ASHERSON, R. 1969. South Africa: Race and Politics. *New Left Review* **53**, Jan.–Feb.: 55.

BLALOCK, H. M. 1967. *Toward a Theory of Minority Group Relations.* New York: Wiley.

BLUMER, H. 1965. Industrialization and Race Relations. In Hunter, G. (ed.), *Industrialization and Race Relations.* London: Oxford University Press.

BUDD, S., & PLATT, J. 1964. Discussion on Social Stratification in Industrial Society. In Halmos, P. (ed.), *The Development of Industrial Societies*, Sociological Review Monograph No. 8.

CARMICHAEL, S. 1968. Black Power. In Cooper, D. (ed.), *The Dialectics of Liberation.* Harmondsworth: Penguin Books.

CARTER, G., KARIS, T., & STULTZ, N. M. 1967. *South Africa's Transkei, The Politics of Domestic Colonialism.* London: Heinemann.

DE KIEWIET, C. W. 1942. *A History of South Africa, Social and Economic.* London: Oxford University Press.

DICKIE-CLARK, H. F. 1966. *The Marginal Situation.* London: Routledge and Kegan Paul.

DOXEY, G. V. 1961. *The Industrial Colour Bar in South Africa.* London: Oxford University Press.

EDUCATIONAL PANEL (The 1961) 1966. Second Report. *Education and The South African Economy.*

FRANK, G. 1967. *Capitalism and Under-Development in Latin America.* New York: Monthly Review Press.

HOBART HOUGHTON, D. 1964. *The South African Economy.* London: Oxford University Press.

HORRELL, M. 1965. *A Survey of Race Relations in South Africa.* South African Institute of Race Relations.

HORRELL, M. 1968. *A Survey of Race Relations in South Africa.* South African Institute of Race Relations.

HORRELL, M. 1969. *South Africa's Workers.* South African Institute of Race Relations.

HORWITZ, R. 1967. *The Political Economy of South Africa.* London: Weidenfeld and Nicholson.

HUTT, W. H. 1964. *The Economics of the Colour Bar.* London: André Deutsch.

KERR, C., HARBISON, F., DUNLOP, J. J., MYERS, C. 1960. *Industrialism and Industrial Man.* Cambridge, Mass.: Harvard University Press.

KUPER, L. 1965. *An African Bourgeoisie.* Yale University Press.

MACCRONE, E. D. 1947. *Race Attitudes in South Africa.* University of Witwatersrand Press.

MARQUARD, L. 1957. *South Africa's Colonial Policy.* South African Institute of Race Relations.

SOUTH AFRICAN COMMUNIST PARTY 1962. The Road to South African Freedom. London: Ellis Bowles.

SPOONER, E. P. 1960. *South African Predicament*. London: Jonathan Cape.

TIRYAKIAN, E. A. 1957. Apartheid and Religion. *Theology Today* **14**: 342.

VAN DEN BERGHE, P. 1967. *South Africa: A Study in Conflict*. University of California Press.

VAN DER HORST, S. 1942. *Native Labour in South Africa*. London: Oxford University Press.

VAN DER HORST, S. 1965. The Effects of Industrialization on Race Relations in South Africa. In Hunter, G. (ed.), *Industrialization and Race Relations*. London: Oxford University Press.

Index